Rise UP
The Soulful Guide to Success

Diane McKendrick

First published by Busybird Publishing 2018
Copyright © 2018 Diane McKendrick

ISBN
Print: 978-1-925830-39-2
Ebook: 978-1-925830-40-8

Diane McKendrick has asserted her right under the Copyright, Designs and Patents Act 1988 to be identified as the author of this work. The information in this book is based on the author's experiences and opinions. The publisher specifically disclaims responsibility for any adverse consequences, which may result from use of the information contained herein. Permission to use information has been sought by the author. Any breaches will be rectified in further editions of the book.

All rights reserved. No part of this publication may be reproduced, stored in or introduced into a retrieval system, or transmitted in any form, or by any means (electronic, mechanical, photocopying, recording or otherwise) without the prior written permission of the author. Any person who does any unauthorised act in relation to this publication may be liable to criminal prosecution and civil claims for damages. Enquiries should be made through the publisher.

Cover image: Jaana-Liisa Brown, Think Tank Solutions
Cover design: Busybird Publishing
Layout and typesetting: Busybird Publishing
Editor: Beau Hillier

Busybird Publishing
2/118 Para Road
Montmorency, Victoria
Australia 3094
www.busybird.com.au

When Diane says at the start of this book to grab a journal and pen ... DO IT IMMEDIATELY!

Before I got to the last chapter, I'd realised that I had written my very own personalised blueprint for success!

This cracker read is packed full of simple wisdom straight from the heart. Diane's writing is down to earth and practical, from her personal and professional experience into my bedside journal for implementation and contemplation.

The interactive exercises where super insightful and helped guide me along on many levels. It's a fun book with soul and a few home truths ... Let's always remember that a 'Doona Day' is essential to wellbeing and 'Mt Washing' is actually one of life's positives.

I loved *Rise UP*'s positive and accepting attitude as I devoured it cover to cover in one sitting. I'll definitely be keeping it on my bedside for top-up inspiration!

~ Kylie O'Brien

For my entire family ...

AND

Every woman I have EVER met and every woman I am yet to meet. This book is for YOU, about you and FROM you.

Diane McKendrick
AUTHOR • SPEAKER • LIFE COACH

DIANEMCKENDRICK.COM

Contents

Introduction	i
1. Start UP: The Power of Getting Grounded	1
2. Juggle UP: How to Keep All the Balls in the Air	11
3. Fill UP: Discover the True You	25
4. Fire UP: Goals with Soul	35
5. Shake UP: Adapt and Grow	39
6. Climb UP: Conquer Mt Washing	51
7. Loved UP: Unlocking Connection	55
8. Cashed UP: Money-manifesting Magician	69
9. Stand UP: Perfect Boundaries	79
10. Guilt DOWN: Eliminate Mother's Guilt	85
11. Power UP: Three Steps to Lift Off	101
Acknowledgements	113
About the Author	115
Diane McKendrick – Speaker	117
Offer 1	119
Offer 2	121
Offer 3	123

Introduction

Welcome to *Rise UP*.

My name is Diane McKendrick and I am a driven, focused, successful businesswoman who is also a soft, nurturing, wise, feminine goddess.

I'm writing this book to show you that you can also do what you love, with people you love, and create an impact in the world, adding value to people's lives and receiving financial abundance. Success means different things to different people and I hope to help you get crystal clear on what it is to you – and help you connect with your internal compass, so you can create and align with your vision of success.

Let's rewind a little bit to give you some insight to who I am, where my journey started and how I've come to be the person I am today.

A shy and tender child, I was always extremely intuitive. My childhood years consisted of school, friends, cousins, sleepovers, sports carnivals and holidays with the family. Nothing out of the ordinary for a young girl from a small town.

At the age of twelve at a swimming carnival, I got spotted by a local swim coach who saw potential in my stroke, my mindset and my nature. I was a gifted athlete; I loved every sport I played and could grasp and perfect anything physical in lightning speed. As an adult, any type of movement still fires my soul!

Fast forward five years and after the countless 4 am rises and daily rhythm – pool, school, back to pool, homework – I won Gold at National Titles: my long term goal. I was also a gifted long distance runner graced with perfect physical attributes, a big heart and a winning, focused determination; I found myself representing Australia for running at the age of fifteen in the USA. The moment my feet hit the ground in USA my soul stirred, and I knew I would travel again.

My parents were working tirelessly back at home to pay for all my National and State uniforms, events and trips. I'd started to receive phone calls from American coaches offering me sponsorships to attend college in California and run. I laughed it off, saying, 'I'm a swimmer, not a runner!'

As I look back at these times, I admire the dedication, commitment and humility of my parents. Never did I feel different; never did I feel better than anybody. My family and my training taught me discipline, leadership, focus and belief. The most important quality this journey taught me was resilience: to keep getting back up and to remember that perceived failures were opportunities to change gears and find another way to succeed. It gave me a finite awareness of my mind–body connection. And an introduction to the world of vibration and energy.

Introduction

As an athlete, I learnt to push harder than anyone else – to stretch more, eat better and train harder than my competitors. I believed if someone else stretched more, ate better, or trained harder than me, then they deserved the win. The quiet, overachieving, perfectionist voice in my head made certain that I would do everything possible to be the athlete who had pushed the hardest. Training the hardest and winning was my metric for success. This deeply ingrained belief served me well in becoming the best performing athlete, but it wasn't as relevant in my journey as a mother, wife and successful entrepreneur.

A knee injury forced me to prematurely end my athletic career (self-sabotage, perhaps) and there were several lost years of spending far too much time with Bundaberg rum, nightclubs and driving through McDonald's. I didn't know who I was anymore and plunged into deep depression and questioning. My first thought every morning for many years was, 'I can't wait to go back to bed tonight.' I dreaded the day. I was scared of myself. I lost any connection I had with my higher self and higher purpose and mindlessly stumbled through my days.

My injury coincided with ending high school. In an effort to escape the societal expectation of attending university (my worst nightmare), I got a few different admin jobs so I could save money to travel. After working a few ad hoc jobs, I backpacked around the world for two years. I met up with friends and family along the way, but mainly I was on my own. My soul was aching to rest, to come home – not the tangible house where my family lived in Australia, but the home of my human vessel.

When I started backpacking, my dear dad dropped me off at the airport that morning and must have sensed my gut-wrenching fear of what I was about to undertake. For the next two years I would live from my backpack and be a travelling nomad. 'What are you running away from?' he asked.

Only now as I write this book do I realise how profound my answer was.

'I'm not running away, I'm running towards the real me.'

To say I was petrified would be an understatement. Feeling electric and anxiety-ridden at the same time, I sobbed the whole flight to Ecuador.

Those years were hard, but also some of the most heart-opening, exciting and soul-stirring times of my life.

On my return home, I realised how I had grown and changed through experiencing life, cultures, people … and when I returned it was like a time warp; it appeared as if nothing had changed for people. So my next big project was to get a 'job' to start saving for my next trip. This was when I got my first proper job in the corporate world … and the start of a very destructive cycle.

I started as a receptionist and over several years of using my 'push, strive, overachieve' pattern, I worked my way through to being a senior manager of several large corporations.

I wore cute executive suits with matching $500 handbags and shoes; I had my keepsake coffee mug poised while balancing a briefcase and mobile phone in the other hand. I was exceptional at my job, getting paid bucket loads with promotions coming regularly. I often fielded calls from other companies trying to dangle the carrot and offering me 'more money' to work for them. I felt successful, and from the outside it appeared I had it all.

The industry was cutthroat, competitive, critical and dishonest. I witnessed co-workers be bullied into nervous breakdowns, feeling so helpless and heartbroken that there was nothing I could do. I saw family businesses go bankrupt while others prospered from it.

One day I woke up

I felt empty and tired, like I lived on the hamster wheel of life. I was reacting to life, reaching for all the things I thought would make me happy – always striving and pushing for more. It was never enough. I was sick, overweight and had a huge void in my life where I dearly wanted a partner, but was trapped in a miserable marriage to my soul-destroying job.

I'm not saying that the entire corporate world is like this. I only know my experience of it – and from the feedback from the hundreds of young professionals who come through my programs and to my retreats. Unfortunately, something similar is within the majority of their experiences.

What I did next was the hardest decision of my life. I didn't take the next promotion – the one I had worked towards my whole life.

In fact, this was the catalyst for me leaving my corporate job altogether and that was one of the hardest times of my life. I'd created an identity around my job, my income – and without it, I didn't know who I was.

Although it was one of the hardest decisions of my life, it has been one of the most fulfilling. It gave me the space to listen to myself again. To stop running on the hamster wheel. To remember what lights my soul on fire; to stand with my feet on the grass, meet the man of my dreams, create a conscious and heart-centred business that can help change the world, raise two amazing little humans … and now to write a book about it and show you how to do the same. My vision of success was changing.

I'm not telling you to quit your job straight away, but if my journey resonates with you, I invite you to think of other possibilities. To invite in opportunities to sit and listen to the stirring of your soul. For example, you can see travel, connection, movement and growth woven through my story – and I can say with absolute certainty that my 'job' now revolves around travel, movement, connection and growth.

I am writing this book for YOU – I want this book to be a starting point for you to start questioning what you're currently doing and what you currently associate with succeeding in life. To create outrageous possibility for you and your family.

Some of you reading this book will be in the same position as I was in the corporate world; others might be stay-at-home mummies, entrepreneurs, business owners or authors. Wherever you are in your journey, this book and community can help you. It will help dig out your gold nuggets, polish them off and melt them into gold bars.

Do you have a belief system or pattern that is keeping you stuck – just like my 'push, strive, overachieve' pattern? It often meant I was the fastest athlete and got me high paying executive roles, but it wasn't what my soul was calling for as I awakened from the fog. It served me in getting gold medals, sponsorships, promotions – but being a mum, wife, business mentor and healer calls for something different. Something softer, more aligned.

In my experience, there is a society consensus that you can either be spiritual and aligned, or you can earn enormous income. There seems to be a separation in doing both. I'm here to bust that myth and give you a guide on how you can run an amazing soul-centred business, or work in the corporate world – and still stay true and aligned to you. To laser-focus your awareness and choose which energy or framework is required moment by moment to create more of what you want in life.

Yes, there are definitely still days and moments I flick into scheduling, blueprints, strategy and logistics – which creates the divine, masculine container for me to then drop into my intuition, feminine flow, nurturing and connection in creating my vision.

The book covers all the tools and strategies I've learnt over the last thirty-eight years, from my training and racing days to my corporate job, where I felt empty, tired and reactive to life and past conditioning. Now I'm running a soulful and successful business as a mum and a wife from home, and being a business mentor to so many other women.

It is my dream that this book and our community will be the firestarter for you to click you off autopilot and have you start asking, 'What else is there? What else can I choose and how can I do that feeling good, aligned and certain?'

This book has been a labour of love. There have been ups and downs; it's been far more emotional than I expected. I'm writing to the woman I was fifteen years ago, and the memory of her can be painful. I want to help you avoid what I went through and share my journey, tools and techniques, to catapult you into a life of your dreams and desires.

Life can get so busy and we can get caught in the rat race. This book isn't about how to stay Zen and sit on the top of a mountaintop for the rest of your life; it's about intertwining the moments of directive, masculine focus and then the soft and nurturing guidance. If you're a female entrepreneur, this book is definitely for you. If you're a female working in the corporate industry, you will also get tons of value from it.

Before we move forward, here are a couple of questions to ponder which will start the juices flowing.

- Ever woken up in the morning and thought: 'Is this all there is?'
- Do you 'earn' income or 'create' it?

As we progress through the book, we'll get into all the juicy goodness of using our intuition and creative mode to create connections, relationships and experiences to move forward with.

The key to success is your consistency and patience over a long period of time. It's not a long process that will take years and years, but I would give yourself a reasonable amount of time, so you can make changes slowly, embedding into your life as new habits. Solid, sustainable change is crucial to enhancing your overall lifestyle.

The promises I need from you when you read this book are:

1. to not compare yourself to others
2. to be gentle and nurturing with yourself
3. to not rush it – take the time to sit with it
4. to believe in YOURSELF!

I am not different to you. You can see that from the beginning of my personal story. I'm just a normal mummy doing my best. Questioning everything and feeling my own feelings. Diving deep and willing to adapt, grow and change because my growth and healing is the growth and healing of the sisterhood collective.

You're not on your own. I have a strong vision and you're part of it. So on the days you don't believe in you, remember: I believe in you!

I know all these things, because I used to read books and would often be filled with fear, dread and darkness that I couldn't follow through with all the things these amazing authors were telling me to do. I have learnt that on my journey, I absorb the information I need at the time. You will pick up the messages and information that you need in that moment. Absorb it with your soul, listen with more than your ears and read with more than your eyes!

This book is a reminder to myself as much as to you all that this is the new way forward. Anecdotally speaking, half of you will start to read this book and leave it unfinished either on your bedside table or in the bookcase. There will be another 20% who finish the book, but don't take any action.

Whether you receive gold nuggets or not from this book is totally okay. The most important thing to me is to anchor for you that every time you see this book – every time you catch a glance of it out of the corner of your eye, in the bookcase or on your bedside table – you get a rush of overwhelming gratitude and love, and a feeling that someone believes in you.

No matter what you're going through in your life, I believe in you. I believe in womanhood, I believe in sisterhood and I believe in human spirit. So if you are a human, this book is for you – I believe in you. Our tribe is creating an international sisterhood of women who are supported and loved, regardless of culture, background, job or your choices in raising your children. You'll be supported and loved and encouraged to show up and '*Rise UP*' to the fullest version of you.

No matter how you feel or where you are in your life when you start this book, I want you to remember: twenty years ago, I was a depressed, anxious, scatty and sad little girl who used to wake up every morning and think, 'I can't wait to go back to bed tonight.' No matter where you are throughout this process, you will be supported to take this journey with love, encouragement and belief.

1. Start UP

The Power of Getting Grounded

If you're reading this book, you're probably either a stay-at-home mum, a high-flying corporate biz chick, a mummy entrepreneur, a female entrepreneur – a wife, daughter, friend (or even an amazing man who has these women in your life). Whatever human suit you wear, you've picked this book up for a reason. You either know me, have met me or heard me speak, resonated with a message on my social media or possibly been gifted this book by a friend. I'm choosing to believe that if you're reading this … you TRUST me and my message.

I want the commitment from you, before you sink into this book, to START today. This transformation into your HIGHER SELF starts right now. Declare to the universe with yourself or a friend bearing witness: 'I choose to change – I choose a new path forward.' This starts today.

The twenty-first century has a lot of us feeling disconnected, flighty and scattered. Add into the mixture TVs, devices, junk food, a lot more mothers in the workforce – and I see our health hitting crisis point. Unless something changes, this generation of children will hit crisis point and there will be an epidemic of health issues, stemming from disconnection and disease. Unless we have this awareness, our environment will prove to be a vicious cycle playing on repeat. It's up to us to bring back awareness, to connect back into natural roots, and to create a different possibility of community, health and connection.

I read a magazine article the other day on 'grounding'. The article explained the importance of removing our shoes and getting our feet on the ground. It was stating how relevant and essential grounding is for optimum health.

I was startled and sad that the world has gotten to a stage where something as elementary and normal as walking barefoot on the ground has become a foreign and taboo habit for so many families. It surprises me that it's so far off a lot of people's radar that there are magazine articles about such a natural, simple act to remind us of the importance of staying connected to nature.

On reading the article, I thought, 'Doesn't everybody know that taking your shoes off and walking on the ground is crucial to mental, physical and spiritual health?'

There's a growing body of scientific evidence which proves that the frequency and vibration that comes up from the earth is what humans need to stay 'grounded' in an increasingly busy and chaotic time of life. I don't know about you, but I don't need the confirmation from any 'research' to know that I feel better after 'time out' connection in nature.

1. Start UP

If this concept has triggered an emotional response for you, because you believe that we need to wear shoes to protect our feet and stay away from 'germs', I invite you to think of it like this. Back in the caveman days, we used to be barefoot constantly; we used to sleep on the ground and climb trees, so we were always close to Mother Nature. By comparison, in the twenty-first century we wear rubber soled shoes, walk on tiles or carpet, sleep on a bed, use computers and digital equipment, watch TV, drive to work, sit in a chair all day and eat food that is not recognised by the body as food. This is not the movement or nutrition our body is designed for.

Yes, our bodies have adapted and evolved to be able to do those things, but the feedback loop of mental illness, gut health issues, anxiety, high blood pressure and so on is at an all-time high. It's so imperative that we get back to nature and put our feet on the ground.

I nearly didn't add this chapter into the book, because I was worried what people would think. A little voice inside me said that if I can help one person shift and change their life, then it's worth it. I've also recognised in my role as a life coach that the people who have the most resistance, criticism or emotional charge towards the topic are the ones who need it the most. So, If you're reading this and thinking, 'What on Earth is she talking about?' I want you to sit quietly by yourself with your shoes off on the grass, sink deep into your own breathing and recognise how your body feels. How your mind feels.

I promise not to tell you 'I told you so'!

Subconsciously, I've always known about grounding, because my cells and soul would naturally feel better after time in nature; unfortunately, I haven't always honoured that knowing and feeling.

Back in the days of my corporate job, I was 'busy': rushing around everywhere, working from 7 am till 7 pm and then coming home and doing more work before going to bed. My sleep was broken from stress – I was looking outside myself for acceptance. You might resonate with this feeling of 'the more I did, the better I felt'. Then the metric would change: how much more could I do, how much more could I make? My mind was in a constant flurry of how, when, push, strive – an old paradigm which doesn't serve me anymore. Being an athlete, entrepreneur, mummy and now author, I sometimes feel this deeply ingrained pattern resurface. This is how I recognise and overcome it:

> 'A tree doesn't have to think about growing,
> it just does.'

I found myself completely disconnected and full of dis-ease: overweight, miserable and like the lights had gone out.

Even during these times, I was drawn to nature. There are so many different opportunities, such as organising work events if you are 'busy'. For example, I used to organise team-building hikes within our organisation. We would all meet at ridiculous o'clock in the morning, drive together to a local mountain and up we would go, one step in front of the other all the way to the top. It's exactly like training for an athletic event, preparing for a big corporate gig or job interview, managing children every day, starting a new job, starting your own business, taking charge of your health or writing a book. Take the next step.

If you're stuck and don't know what the next step is, then kick your shoes off and wander barefoot on Mumma Earth. Listen closely; she will give you the answer.

I would go on weekend camping and canoeing trips – some of these memories are my fondest. Bonds and connections formed and it energises you from the inside out.

A hint about overcoming the 'I'm too busy' excuse: the moment I think, 'I'm too busy, or I don't have time,' is the hint that it's time to ground again.

Go get grounded, sister

This is a shout out from the mountaintop to all you stay-at-home mummies, high-flying corporate biz chicks, mummy entrepreneurs, female entrepreneurs and any divine masculine reading this book.

Find some space to ground every single day. I know in the winter months, when I forget to do it and it's dark and cold and the grass is wet, and I don't go out there, I definitely can feel a difference in my body and in my spirit.

As parents, we all want to create and hold space to raise happy, healthy, well adjusted children. Grounding is essential for the wellbeing of your children. Let's start them young and make it a natural part of their daily habits. Let's remind them so early that it becomes a natural part of who they are and what they do.

Watch your children's behaviour after they've been able to run around barefoot and play in the grass – and then watch them through winter when they've had to wear shoes all the time and they're disconnected, scatty or flighty. Sometimes when my two little ones start to get heightened, it's just a matter of taking off their shoes and letting them run outside and play in the dirt.

Some of you might be thinking, 'This sounds crazy, how can walking on the grass possibly help heal myself or my children of grief, overwhelm, anxiety or serious disease?' I'm not saying it's a cure for anything, but what I do know is that it's an important piece of a much bigger puzzle. If you start to do this, it will help create the space to make other, bigger changes in your life. It will be the catalyst to feeling better and taking the next step.

Keep it simple

I don't want to minimise what you're feeling or what's going on for you. People question this concept, as it seems so simple. YES, it is so simple! So simple, in fact, that for some reason the human race likes to complicate it. One thing I can guarantee you is that if you take your shoes off, walk on the earth and slow your breathing down, you will feel better. You'll find yourself in a clearer place, feel connected to your higher self and be ready to take on the next step. Do this with intention and clarity and it will be the launching pad for magnificent possibilities in your health, career, relationship, finance and connections.

There have been so many times in my practice when people have come to me at complete breaking point, completely anxiety-ridden or in deep depression, overwhelm, trauma or grief. Sometimes it's the last resort before turning to synthetic medication or extensive surgery. I have many natural tools, strategies and techniques I offer to people, but when you get to a certain threshold or breaking point where your spirit is separating from your body, there is a very small window … especially if you're not coping with life and you have a job and children to look after. You feel trapped in the hamster wheel.

I know because I've been at breaking point, and I'm lucky to have a supportive family, great natural therapists, an incredible husband and nurturing friends to support me through tough times.

If you're having an out-of-body experience and separating from yourself, it can be really frightening. For myself, clients and friends, my first go-to is to take people outside to get their shoes off and walk on the grass.

To be honest, I used to cringe because for a long time that voice in my head would be critical that I couldn't do any 'textbook technique' and that someone paid me a full consultation fee to literally take their shoes off and walk on the grass.

Every single time I taught or reminded someone of this process, I had to override the voice in my head and listen to my soul. Then I reflect on the look in these women's eyes and the way they dropped back into their bodies – and that they could breathe again, slow down. The feedback they've given me is that it feels like a homecoming, like all the things they've learnt to 'be' and the masks they need to wear to 'feel worthy' all dissipate into Mother Nature.

This is my mission: to remind you of your power, to bring you home to yourself and do life from this place.

Regardless of how loud the criticism and judgment coming from the voice in my head or from society – yes, I've had my fair share of tall poppy syndrome, with people directing their negativity towards me – I care more now about your health and wellbeing than what people think of me. I'm going to continue to share from my heart and soul to your heart and soul. I'll share my journey of my family, my life and my business. I'll share how I stay grounded and centred in a fast-paced, sometimes competitive, destructive business world.

> **Essential Oil: Myrrh, Oil of Mother Earth**
>
> Apply to feet and throat before grounding; when you wear or diffuse, it will trigger the response and memory of homecoming.

Play time

While we're discussing non-conventional ideas, child's play has been extraordinary for me. When I'm starting to feel overwhelmed or stressed, I'll spend a couple of minutes watching my daughter, Esme, or a small child play – and then I'll mimic their behaviours.

It's absolutely freeing to run like a three year old, with arms flailing out to the sides, the head moving forward, the little grin on your face and the little screams of glee. You don't have to do it in public, but I have before and all that's happened is everybody around me has giggled. It really is fulfilling and so connective when I'm running around like that and Esme looks at me like it's the most normal thing in the world for her mum to be like this.

It's time to remember the fun parts of your childhood. Remember how to play in complete innocence, love and joy – the time before ego took hold of us. Before we learnt to be scared; before we learnt to compete and strive, argue, to question and criticise ourselves, to judge ourselves and others. Let's revisit that place and settle in for a while. This energy will transfer over to your business, relationships, finances and health.

1. Start UP

You'll embody a certain sense of calm, gratitude and peace when people talk to you. You'll feel different around people; they won't be able to put it into words, but they'll feel different around you as well. They'll know to trust you and that you bring out the beauty, childlike humour and fun in them.

Life and business is about the way you FEEL, and the impact you contribute to and create in other human lives. Don't take yourself too seriously and always remember to have fun.

2. Juggle UP

How to Keep All the Balls in the Air

Let's paint a picture. I'm certain you will relate to this, possibly even have a giggle. I like to call it the dinnertime rush.

Gus is away for several days on end and I'm in the kitchen trying to make a healthy meal to keep the kids healthy – something they like, something I like. The cat's around my feet trying to get fed and the kids are yelling out from the bath that they need soap, or are starting to have an argument on whose toy belongs to whom. In the middle of that, my phone is dinging, flashing, vibrating with Facebook messages, text messages, emails, comments from friends, family and followers asking for advice and guidance. I'm trying to book in appointments, babysitting schedules, homework updates and deal with overdue library books.

I dash in to check on the kids between mashing sweet potato and cooking green beans, and I notice they've covered the bathroom from floor to ceiling with bath water. I have a fleeting moment of mixed frustration at having to clean up the floor ... but they are content and playing nicely again.

I grab the dirty clothes that lay thrown across the floor (in an effort to save dirtying clean towels and adding to Mt Washing). I bundle the dirty clothes into a pile and try to soak up the water. Now I hear the green beans boiling over, my phone is vibrating itself off the bench and looks like a fireworks display, the cat is meowing louder and ... it's only 6 pm.

This is fondly nicknamed 'dinnertime rush' at my place. It is hectic. Regardless of how prepared or relaxed I am, how much (or how loud) I play meditation music, the deep breaths I take or essential oils I diffuse and pour over myself, the kids and the cat in preparation for the dinnertime rush ... I've realised on some level, this time of our day is heightened. I need to rise to meet it, whether I'm willing and ready, or not!

How do you do it all?

One of the questions I get asked the most is, 'Di, how do you do it all?'

Here is my honest answer: 'Sometimes I nail it and mostly, I don't.'

The next little piece of advice is one of the most profound things you're ever going to read or hear. IT'S OKAY TO DROP THE BALL. If we go back to the vision of the mum in the kitchen juggling all those important things – how to make food, how to keep it healthy, how to reply to everyone, how to be everything to everyone – remember, it's okay to drop the ball. You don't have to keep all the balls in the air at all times.

2. Juggle UP

What this chapter is not going to tell you is how to juggle like a pro and keep all those balls in the air at once. What I will offer is an authentic and real message, from my heart to yours, on how I do the balancing act of being mum, wife, daughter, entrepreneur and all the other hats that I wear on a daily basis, staying connected to my higher self and purpose.

I hope my experience and insights will gift you with some valuable tools, tips and tricks – if you adopt them, you'll get to know yourself on a different level and create a sustainable and ethical approach to the tightrope walk of personal and business life.

I feel like the world has taken us to a place where mums are supposed to work, be the perfect wife, have the perfect body, be the perfect mum, look after our parents if they're sick or old … and take on everything that comes with that.

We have created a culture where material things matter; we over-commit and extend our important resources. If this has any chance of changing, we all need to take responsibility for how we show up in it. As a collective, we need to become present and aware and start to prioritise. To dig deeper and uncover your core values so you can prioritise the important things and let the rest slide. You will discover a new, deep sense of self for you and your needs.

What is your glass overflowing with?

The fuller that you are, the fuller everybody else is around you. Imagine your body, heart and soul as a cup: if we fill it up with stress, anxiety, depression and feelings of inadequacy, when that cup is full, it overflows with the darkness and chaos, which filters out to everybody around you.

Likewise, if we fill our cup with love, joy, intention and purpose, then when the cup gets full and overflows, what filters out to everybody else is a sense of love, purpose and connection.

Grab your journal and draw your cup. Fill it with colour, creativity and all the desires and feelings you want more of. Put it up somewhere you see regularly to remind you to fill your cup with the good stuff.

Breaking point

Most of you reading this have had an experience in your life where you've felt the strong arms of emptiness, sadness and overwhelm embrace you with vigorous constriction. Perhaps you're even feeling that now? Everyone has a threshold; you know your threshold and the internal clues and hints your mind and body give you when it's sneaking up on you. You need to establish a game plan to navigate it BEFORE you reach it. Once you've hit it and gone into meltdown mode, it's an uphill struggle to claw your way back.

With all the extra pressures of today, if you choose to excel in business (or not), I guarantee that there will come a time when you feel at breaking point. When you consider the contrast of highs and lows, personal pressure and expectation we commit to, it's a similar environment to a pressure cooker. Which, when the heat is turned high enough, will eventually erupt.

One thing that will release the valve on the pressure cooker is to let go of expectations. Release the ideas, concepts and images that society places on you. The expectations in your own head and the judgment of the people around you are a distraction from the important messages.

One of the most powerful support tools for this is the community. We have an international tribe of women who are here to remind you that you're not alone. You are not home alone during the dinnertime rush. There are other woman and families all over the world doing the dinnertime rush, pulling their hair out, wondering, 'How did I get myself stuck into this mess?'

Unfortunately, it's come to my attention through my own experience (and the thousands of clients I've worked with) that adrenal fatigue and family breakdowns are at an all-time high because we're spreading ourselves too thin. We're distracting ourselves with the daily to-do list, leaving people feeling empty, disconnected and trapped. I can speak from personal experience that trying to be everything to everybody, and keeping everybody happy all of the time, will not work long term. For a long time I felt like a mindless robot on repeat or a hamster on a wheel: the faster I ran, the faster it spun.

Eventually I got to a point where I had to make some drastic changes, because my physical and mental health was compromised. I had fallen clean from the tightrope of life and luckily was caught by a safety net, giving me a second chance at life and business.

It is my mission to help you make some changes before you erupt or get coaxed back into the strong embrace of emptiness and endless questioning – before you hit your threshold (or rock bottom, as some would call it), or your body gets dis-ease or your relationship breaks down, or your business goes belly up.

In nature, back in the early days, our adrenaline was there to protect us. For example, if you were getting chased by a tiger, you want that adrenaline to spike to alert you that there's a threat there. In this modern life, the ding of the phone, the beep on the email, children's temper tantrums and financial burdens become that tiger. That meeting at work with the boss becomes that tiger. That idiot in traffic who just cut you off becomes that tiger. So, in all those examples, you have the physiological rise of the adrenaline that's there to protect you. But our body doesn't know the difference between actually being attacked by something and going into protection mode, or just being a perceived threat.

Many of us live our life in that red zone, with our adrenaline getting pumped through our body daily. Add coffee, relationship issues or money woes, a constant feeling of not being good enough ... and you have a ticking time bomb. A pressure cooker full to the brim, getting the gauge turned right up.

This quote sums it up perfectly:

> *'The ego says, once everything falls into place, I'll feel at peace. But spirit says, find your peace and then everything will fall into place.'*
>
> Marianne Wiliamson

It's time to stop striving and pushing, and replace that with alignment awareness and presence. I promise that if you approach your life this way, it will evolve and transform into something fun and extraordinary. This is my metric for success now.

Honour your cycle

We must honour that we are cyclic beings. As human beings we all have a natural blueprint. Sometimes through the month I feel like connecting, getting out and hosting workshops, presenting as guest or key note speaker at large events or hosting my own events. Other times I wake up and feel like I'm so introverted and painfully shy, even ordering a coffee is a struggle; I want to lock myself away and hide.

For a long time, I thought something was wrong with me. I thought I had some sort of personality disorder that separated me from the rest of the world. I found myself locking myself away even on the days where I felt good.

Neither of these states are good or bad. The contrast is vast and I am open to exploring deeper. I invite you to also investigate and shine some light on your high vibrational states and lower vibrational states, and the meaning you may have subconsciously attached to them.

I used to think when I was in my 'lower vibe' I was less productive, as I wasn't 'getting stuff done'. There was nothing I could tick off my 'to-do list' because even monotonous, easy everyday tasks, which I usually do with ease, became a challenge. It's just the way it is. Some days I'm tuned in, driven, focused, connected and orientated – and other days I want to retreat to a dark bedroom, cover my head with the pillow and stay there … for as long as it takes.

I can guarantee that everyone reading this, men and woman, would have and still will experience these cycles and contrasts. Firstly, you must recognise how you feel and be willing to shine light on it. Don't get caught in the trap of 'always feeling good'; it's easy to trick yourself into this. Especially in the twenty-first century: the world of instant gratitude and constant internet connection, and the billion dollar industry convincing us at every corner that we need to be sunshine and rainbows all the time to feel happy, valued and content.

Add 'Doona day' to your to-do list

Give yourself permission to have a 'doona day'. To go back to bed, close the curtains, pull the doona over your head and cry, or read, or just lay. No personal development, no questioning, no audio books or podcasts, no social media ... just you and your doona. Write 'Doona Day' on your to-do list RIGHT NOW!

I woke up one morning and for no apparent reason, felt like rubbish. The old me would have puffed my chest, thrown myself into my to-do list, put on my 'badge of busy', convinced myself with positive affirmations and played upbeat music LOUD. She would have kept pushing and pretending. Something deeper in me stirred and I asked myself, 'What would it feel like if I just went back to bed?'

My ego launched into a flurry of questioning. On that day there was a higher power at play and the message was loud and clear: close the curtains, go back to bed and pull the doona over your head. I asked my husband, Gus if he could do all the 'kid stuff' and I retreated underneath the doona. I laid there for twenty minutes thinking of little, letting the negative self-talk run rampant through my mind. I cried for nothing and everything at the same time.

After about an hour, I rolled over and to my surprise, I just started laughing at myself; laughing at the pure release and freedom I felt by giving myself time to retreat, recharge and recalibrate. My mind chatter returned to, 'What a beautiful day. Why am I lying in bed, when I could be out enjoying that?' So I stayed there for a little longer in rest and recalibrate mode; when I felt ready, I jumped up, opened the curtains and entered my day feeling like a newly cleaned whiteboard: once covered in crazy, heavy drawings, art and emotion but now a gleaming white space of possibility and creation.

Previously I would have 'soldiered on' until I hit boiling point, or created a drama, dis-ease or event in my life so I could have a rest or use it as an excuse to stop. The pure action of allowing myself to stop meant that the process lasted a few hours instead of an unknown amount of time, in response to whatever emotional turmoil I put myself through.

The message here is, catch your cycles and give yourself permission to retreat and relax when you need to. Don't keep pushing just because your ego is driving your decisions.

This makes perfect sense when I relate it back to nature. If an animal has just given birth or been hurt, that creates the stress hormone cortisol; it's natural, as is the animal licking their wounds and recuperating in a dark, safe and comfortable place. It is even more relevant these days, as cortisol (the 'tiger chasing you' hormone) is pulsating through most people's veins daily.

The awareness starts by stopping – by slowing down, dropping into your body, becoming ultra-conscious of how it's feeling and listening to its messages. It's something I do daily, and you can too. It's as simple as taking a single second to check in: scanning down your body and noticing where any tension and tightness is residing, then taking a deep breath and sending light to that place.

Where are you saying YES where you could be saying NO?

If you're juggling several balls and someone asks you to juggle one more, if you overextend and you say YES when you really mean NO, the whole lot can come crashing down. It would have been better to say NO in the first place! Not only is it okay to say NO, it is non-negotiable to check in with yourself and make a call on what is right for you.

I know from experience and from working with so many of you that the pattern and pain of saying YES, when you really mean NO, wreaks havoc on lives. It seems like such a simple concept but for some reason we make it so hard for ourselves.

Saying YES to everybody else is saying NO to yourself, and as we discussed earlier, who is the most important person in the world? We think by saying yes all the time we are helping people, but the best way we can help them is by being the fullest, healthiest and most honest version of ourselves. If you crash and burn because you've taken too much on and said YES when you meant NO, who is going to look after your children, your partner, your business? Let's prioritise your health and set clear boundaries … and we start that by practising saying NO!

Go through your diary or your schedule right now and book in time for yourself, as you do with clients or friends. I know most of you wouldn't cancel on a client or on a friend for a coffee date, but you also have to schedule time in for yourself.

I hear some of you saying, 'I can't say no. If I say no, who's going to do it? It's not going to get done.' I had so much resistance to this when I first heard it, but do you know how empowering it was the first time I said no to somebody because I had a date with myself? You wouldn't cancel on a client or customer, so DON'T CANCEL ON YOURSELF.

The first time I said no, the sky didn't part and strike me down with lightning. No, my leg didn't fall off. Basically, the person said 'okay' and life carried on. It was such a pivotal point in my life where I realised I had the power. I am the director of my own life.

Exercise

That is your homework for this week. Say 'no' to somebody when you would usually say yes. Do it with grace, connection and love.

If you just can't bring yourself to say no, because the emotional charge is too much, gently observe yourself in that moment. Note how it feels in your body if your head is saying, 'No, I don't want to do it,' but the words that come out of your mouth are, 'Yes, it's okay, I'll do it.' It will lead to feeling resentful, annoyed at that person and, worst of all, annoyed at yourself. It then becomes a vicious cycle.

If you feel this is too much of a jump in the deep end, let's take baby steps. Rewind slightly, observe yourself in the conversation and if you don't have the courage to verbally say NO, just imagine yourself saying no from a place of love and gratitude. Ask yourself, 'What's the worst that can happen if I say no?'

I promise King Kong will not swing from the closest tallest building and take you hostage!

Start saying yes to yourself, booking in time and scheduling around it. If you follow this process, you will gently and confidently build yourself up to saying no when you mean no and yes when you mean yes. A very empowering quality indeed.

If you still find this a difficult concept, life has a magical way of creating things if you ask. Simply ask for guidance.

Ask for help

To be able to juggle all the things that I do, I've also had to learn to ask for and receive help. Asking is one thing and receiving is another. I always used to think I was really good at asking and receiving help ... until I actually needed it. That was a huge reality check. It was conditional for me; I realised I could receive when I asked for it and someone gave me something, but when I was backed into the corner and felt like I was empty and needed help, that's when it was hard to receive.

I might hear some of you saying, like when I first heard this, 'But I'm always the one to help. People will think I'm not coping if I ask for help.' Think of it like this: how good does it feel to help somebody? We all want to help somebody; it's part of our DNA and it seems unusual to me that it's so easy to help somebody, yet not so easy to receive help.

Pick a close friend or an 'accountability buddy' and do it: ask for help and then receive. If you give people an opportunity to help you, it will light them up. If they decide it's not for them or it's crossing their boundaries, or they don't want to, then it's up to them to say no and set their boundaries. But let's make this commitment here, with each other, to ask for help. You're always willing to help someone else and there's always someone there ready to help you.

Going back to the picture of me at home in the kitchen with my hair everywhere, the cat around my legs, the kids having a disagreement in the bath, my phone constantly going ding, ding, ding, the dinner burning, my breath short – and you know the rest. Just know that you are not alone. It's okay to drop the ball. There's good days and bad days, so let's just focus on having more good than bad. Also know that on the bad days, we can learn from our experiences. Let's teach our children that it's okay not to be perfect. It's okay to be real, it's okay to be human and it's okay to drop the ball.

In fact, it's okay to drop all the balls. This is your life and you have the choice. Pick up the balls that matter to you in that moment and juggle those. Let's facilitate growth, certainty, love and a mindset of looking after each other and creating your life instead of responding to it. You choose your balls – it's your life.

Create life – Stop reacting to it

My dream is to bring women together to live in their fullest potential. When I do that, it gives permission for others to do the same; it filters into the community and gives everybody the permission to stand in their own power and make their own decisions, to create life instead of reacting to it. If you don't feel full in your personal life, it will definitely reflect in your business. Stay true to yourself.

> ### Essential Oil: Balance
> Apply to feet and diffuse.

3. Fill UP

Discover the True You

Outcomes in your life are a reflection of YOU

Are you working *in* your business or *on* your business? If you wake up feeling drained, frustrated and like you're struggling to make ends meet, then this chapter is for you.

Likewise, you might find your business is skyrocketing, but you spend endless nights losing sleep, find it hard to make decisions or wake up feeling tired and empty most mornings.

Your business, body, relationships and finances are all a reflection of what is happening on the inside. If you predominately have feelings of lack, scarcity, inadequacy, abandonment and anger, these will show up in other areas of your life. Your life will improve when you take personal responsibility for what's happening on the inside and heal that first.

Let's explore how feeling connected and full can enhance your business and life.

Do what you love

The first step to running a soulful business while staying true and authentic to you is to connect with something you love – to create a heart-centred, conscious business that thrives by creating an impact and doing something that matters to YOU. This will help you feel full, empowered and activated.

If you're currently in a job or own a business that doesn't speak to your soul, it will be a challenge to get the drive, vision and focus required to take your business to the next level, or to get the next promotion.

Don't feel defeated if you're in a role that doesn't resonate with you. It is serving some purpose in your life right now. Honour the journey and open up your heart and mind to what else is out there, waiting for you.

Ask yourself right now:

- What lights you up?
- What gives you goosebump moments?
- What brings you joy?
- What did you love to do when you were a child?
- What do you spend time doing that causes you to lose track of time?
- What would you do if money wasn't a consideration?

Digging deeper and pondering these questions will help you start to identify what you enjoy in life. It's surprising when I ask my first-time clients these questions; the majority of them stare back at me blankly, as if I just asked them to cut off their leg.

The reason for this is because most of us are operating on autopilot. In the past I was so distracted by 'being busy'. It meant I didn't have to sit with uncomfortable feelings. I subconsciously used it as an excuse to avoid unravelling the painful thoughts, ideas, memories or beliefs about myself. We are master magicians at avoiding what we are really thinking and feeling, especially if it's perceived as painful.

Even as I write this, I can see a few of your nodding your head in agreement. It is such a common trait among us. I still find myself in this pattern. Now, I have a team of mentors and accountability buddies, and the strategies I'm sharing in this book to assist me in recognising these moments and to dive deep, be honest and move forward with ease and grace.

Monday morning mindset

Have a look on Monday morning when you drive to work or on the train or bus. Take a sideways peek at the driver or passenger beside you. Do they looked eager and pumped, focused and infused with enthusiasm to be traveling to work? Or do most of the people you witness look dull, lifeless, depressed and bored, like they're just going through the motions?

Now, which one are you? If I was driving/sitting beside you and glanced over your way, would you be dull and bored, dreading the day, or would the exchange be vibrant and energetic, a smile perhaps, maybe even a wave? Are you the driver who chooses your music with awareness, sings loudly and does outrageous dance moves, or listens mindlessly to the doldrums of the depressing news?

Your drive or transit to work is a POWER POINT in your day. You choose and set your state for the day. Every day, regardless of what is going on in my life, I choose awareness while I drive to my office. It is only a twenty minute drive for me but I spend that time reflecting on blockages, and I do EFT tapping while I drive (more about that in the last chapter). I choose podcasts or audiobooks that activate, empower and inspire me and I choose music that gives me goosebumps and throws me into a flurry of wild theatrical dance moves. I sing so loud my voice is often strained by the time I get there. Even that vision gives me a giggle!

By the time I get to work I'm 'flying high on life'. I'm sure my colleagues and clients feel the difference on the days I do this and the days I don't. I know my productivity and body knows the difference!

When I used to work from my office at home, I had a similar ritual to go into the headspace for 'work'. Therefore, if you work from home, you don't get out of the crazy wild woman dance moves. Turn it up and start creating, Sister!

Depressive feelings are common

I don't want to minimise people's experience with depression, but it is near impossible to feel dark and depressed when you are listening to a pumping song, sniffing Wild Orange essential oil, singing (badly) really loudly, commuting to a job you love with people you love, and working on a mission and vision that fills you right up. It tricks the neurones in your brain into releasing serotonin, which is the happy hormone.

It's common for a normal, average human being to experience bouts of depression throughout their life. Therefore, in my opinion it is normal to experience this state and these feelings at least a few times in your life. However, the difference is some of us have tools, strategies, techniques, relationships and frameworks to get through it, and others do not.

Society has a negative perception towards depression, but I believe events and emotions normally perceived as negative or painful have an important role in our life. They arise to let us know we are out of alignment and we need to make some changes to get back on purpose. I also work with a lot of people who have grief- and trauma-related states and experiences of post-traumatic stress.

If you have something you need extra support on, please reach out to a professional who can help you through these times.

Dreams are meant to be lived

If you just close your eyes and stay on autopilot, you'll find yourself floating through life, reacting to situations and having depressive thoughts which filter into negative choices, negative relationships and an empty life. A destructive cycle.

I hope to inspire every single one of you to feel aligned and purposeful. When you're 'on purpose' in life, you can create your dreams. Dreams are made to be lived. Many of us think that dreams are just in our head, but I'm here to show you that dreams are meant to be reality.

My dream is to bring women together to live to their fullest and highest potential – to hold them at their highest vibration and always see them in their brightest light. When I do that, it gives permission for others to do the same ... and when you do that, it gives permission for everybody around you to feel their own light (and yours).

When you go out into the world, a vibration transcends and infiltrates into the community. But if you don't feel full, then it will reflect in your business. Stay true to yourself, always ask questions, wake up with purpose and live every day with passion, creativity and curiosity.

I've given you a few things that could help you along the way, but I'd really like to explore further into two clear practices that you can start immediately. I know you're all busy mums or business owners, so I don't want to give you more to do. I want to set the framework for you to shift and change your thoughts and feelings in your own reality.

Power point of your day

What is the first thought through your head in the morning? The very moment when you open your eyes, before you get up and go to the toilet, before you start thinking about what's on in the day – what is that first thought through your mind?

For a really long time, my first thought in my head was, 'I can't wait to go back to bed tonight.' How depressing is that? The day that followed was usually dark, miserable, unproductive and stagnant for me.

Your moment of waking is a POWER POINT for your day, because that very sliver of time creates your state for the day. If you can choose your state in that moment, it's likely to transfer throughout the day. All these days together equal your life, so it's fair to say you can change your life by having awareness and choosing love, abundance, gratitude, community, passion and purpose in your POWER POINT.

If you wake up and you're writing a mental list of things to do, the pattern is overwhelm, rush and feeling like you never get enough done. If you wake up and you're pressing 'snooze, snooze, snooze', then the pattern is procrastination and that's what follows through for the rest of the day.

If you do nothing else as a result of reading this book, visiting that moment in the morning and having awareness and consciousness around it will change your life. It will change your connection with yourself and your family, and it will change the outcomes in your business or at work.

Should vs could

Another simple and effective strategy is changing the word 'should' to 'could'. How does it feel if I say to you, 'You should wash your car today'? And then you don't do it. How do you feel?

If I change that language and said to you, 'You could wash your car today if you wanted to,' how does that feeling change? Did you notice there was a flick in the way that you felt?

I do this with a lot of my clients. When you say 'could', it empowers you to make a choice. And then even if you decide not to do it, you're not feeling guilty; you just made a choice not to do it. Once again, it seems like something so simple, but it's so relevant and so profound – it's something that we can do without adding more things to our to-do list.

Make clear decisions

As a business owner, a mum, a wife and all the other hats we wear, we have a lot of decisions to make. If you're feeling full, aligned and on purpose, you will have clarity and resilience around setting solid boundaries, making important decisions and moving in the direction that is important to you, creating momentum and magic in all areas of your life. If you're uncertain and unsure, you'll be pushed around and moulded by the people who are clear and focused on their vision.

If you're confident and comfortable with the person you are, you will thrive on all levels and give yourself a springboard to jump out of your comfort zone. Being out of the comfort zone is where the magic happens. If you just float along every day feeling comfortable, nothing will change. It takes change to create further change. It takes courage to change.

When you step into full alignment, choose abundance over scarcity, choose belief in yourself over fear and doubt. You will start to feel at peace with yourself and your decisions; you'll move forward with success in your business, home, health and relationships.

When living your life from this space, you will enjoy and transfer high vibrational states such as joy, hope, trust, abundance, inspiration and possibility to all the people who come into contact with your product, service or self.

I feel passionate about this and I've seen it work thousands of times – these are some of the strategies I always come back to. When I'm pushed up against my boundaries or I'm being challenged, I have created a tribe of people around me now who give me a big smile, a hug and remind me of these simple things.

In writing this book I realise I've created the most loving, beautiful tribe of people that reflect back to me the love, the gratitude, the tools and the techniques that help me feel full and loved ... and like I'm making a difference in this world. If you're ready to make a difference in this world, welcome to the tribe.

> **Essential Oil – Geranium, Oil of Trust**
>
> Apply to heart space.

4. Fire UP

Goals with Soul

What is your experience with goal setting? It's a buzzword bandied around the personal development world. Goal setting is important in your forward momentum, although I feel a huge, delicious slice of the pie has been missed. I see many people on 'achievement auto-pilot'.

Initially I was taught the SMART method. I have it on post-it notes, scrawled in notepads, written on the white board and carved into my memory. It stands for Specific, Measurable, Attainable, Relevant and Timely. This method has been helpful to me and so many others, so don't discount it.

However, I have discovered something when combined with this it's even more powerful! I've had my own achievements and watched family, friends and colleagues thrive on 'achievement auto-pilot', accomplishing some outrageous, amazing results by using this or similar techniques. I've witnessed motivation, discipline, sacrifice and a pure push to 'achieve'. Nearly as many times, I've watched as people have arrived at their goal still feeling lost, lonely, empty – asking, 'What's next?'. I know because this has also happened to me.

Most of us have been taught to set goals and then take action steps to get there. To fiercely pursue the goal at all costs. How often have you gotten to a goal and still felt empty? I know in my own experiences there's been plenty of times when I've pushed and strived to reach a goal, only to get there and say, 'What's next?'

> *'It's not about the goal, it's about how you feel when you get there.'*
>
> Danielle LaPorte

In this chapter, we'll be exploring setting goals with soul, deeply connecting into that internal compass and being navigated by what feels good and what feels right. I find even a shift in the word 'goal' to 'intention' helps me connect to my deeper meaning. If you're ever in a position in business or in your family life where something doesn't feel right, then don't do it.

Let's shift the word 'push' to being 'pulled' to a feeling you desire. When you focus on the feeling you want more of, chasing goals becomes living them. Ask yourself, 'What can I do today to feel this way?' We are reverse engineering which is a very practical and successful strategy. What do your goals need to look like, to feel the way you want to feel? You may notice that even asking these questions will provide enormous revelations for you.

Some people get distracted by the dollar signs, a potential promotion or the potential fame and fortune, only to end up

4. Fire UP

feeling empty, wanting and distracting themselves by chasing the next goal.

This is where your goals with soul, or setting solid intentions with depth and commitment, will help you feel certain and complete about your future and that you're on the right path and creating an impact on the world.

Think about what really gets you pumped up. This is your firestarter: that feeling in the belly, or conversations you have with friends or family members that get you really passionate. Things that you lay awake at night thinking about, or charities or places to which you'd like to contribute. When you find something that you're excited about and reconnect with that purpose and that passion, you will be amazed. You'll be pulled towards it instead of pushing to 'get it'.

Carve out time to sit down and set solid, soulful intentions that move you. Connect with feelings and set goals that stir emotion in you, because it's bigger and deeper than you.

Set intentions that create an impact and make a contribution to the world. I know from experience that promotions, money, fame and fortune all have your ego pat you on the back and say, 'Good job.' But the real changes occur when you operate from a higher frequency, encourage yourself to serve others and guide them in doing the same by feeling fulfilled, healthy and aware.

When you go to sleep at night, how do you feel? Do you feel like you've been of full service to humanity? Do you feel like you're contributing and the fire in your belly has started?

Ask yourself, if you had all the money in the world, what would you spend your time doing? Make changes in your life so you can transition into this lifestyle, and I guarantee that your life, relationships, business, health and career will transform.

> **Essential Oil – Passion**
>
> Apply to pulse points and wear as perfume.

5. Shake UP

Adapt and Grow

If you want to THRIVE in life and biz, first you must learn to adapt.

> 'It's not the strongest of the species that survives, nor the most intelligent, it is the one that is most adaptable to change.'
>
> Charles Darwin

Does anyone else find themselves doing something over and over and over again, only to have it not work? This chapter is a tribute to my old self, to that young lady who used to rush around doing everything for everybody else – because it's all she knew.

I believe all humans do the best they can with what they have; we make conscious and subconscious decisions every moment because, whether we recognise it or not, we believe it will bring us a recognised feeling which we associate with 'comfort'.

Unfortunately, the feelings we associate with comfort aren't always positive, uplifting and empowering. We are wired to gravitate towards and repeat past patterns. Awareness, clarity and being able to adapt and change your direction are unavoidable if you're a conscious being who is cultivating a flourishing business and lifestyle.

Your past experiences, perceptions and beliefs of those experiences will regulate your subconscious choices. If your younger years were fraught with questioning, arguments, manipulation and feeling unsafe – or that your human needs for survival weren't met – you may find yourself stuck in subconscious patterns of self-sabotage. Ultimately, you feel fundamentally flawed on a deep level, so to feel safe or comfortable you revert to patterning which you picked up and internalised as a young child.

Likewise, you may have had the 'perfect' upbringing but still find yourself in patterns of self-sabotage. This is because of how you perceived or internalised the world around you as a young child. Although re-running these patterns is painful, it's what your brain is wired to do … and humans as a whole resist change.

Unless something changes, nothing will change.

How many of you out there, like me a few years ago, wake up every morning and continue to do the same thing? Do you think the same thoughts, take the same action and expect different outcomes, and then get all sorts of frustrated when nothing changes? It's a long, destructive, disheartening cycle. It's a scarcity mindset, a deep longing for something more fulfilling.

If you find yourself in that cycle, it's time to become your own observer – catch your thoughts, feelings and emotions, and then switch them around to something more desirable. Your brain is like a computer and memories are its data. It's as simple as pressing eject on the undesirable movie and replacing it with a more empowering, compelling, captivating script.

Firstly, you need the awareness to recognise when something's not working for you, and secondly, the courage to change it. Humans generally don't like change. I've tricked myself many times into thinking that I adapt to change really well, but to be honest, every time I've been pushed to my threshold and had to change the way that I think, feel or interact, I'm challenged, because it's human instinct. Survival is based on being able to adapt.

If you're reading this chapter, nodding your head and saying to yourself, 'Is she writing about me?' you're not on your own.

Regardless of how things manifest into our reality, when things are stripped back there are several fundamental elements which are at the foundation of these behaviours. They manifest into our reality in different ways, but ultimately there are fundamental beliefs at the core that are responsible for these thoughts and feelings.

One of these fundamental elements is the lack of direction or not knowing exactly what you want. Before anything in your life will change, you need to have a clear, specific and persistent vision of your destination – ask yourself, 'What do I really want?'

Exercise

Pick an area of your life you would like some momentum in: health, relationships, career, finances, contribution or spirituality.

Write the topic you chose at the top of a page in your journal; underneath that, write, 'What do I really want?' Spend up to ten minutes filling the page with juicy possibilities of what you really want.

Take a break – grab a drink and go to the bathroom – and then continue to read on.

I want you to revisit what you have just written and notice the dialogue you have used.

Most people, when they do this (including myself), respond with dialogue around WHAT THEY DON'T WANT. It sounds something like this: 'Oh my gosh, I don't want to wake up sick and tired any more, I don't want to go to a job where my boss pushes me around, I'm so sick of my husband and kids disrespecting me, I don't want to worry about money or getting my bills paid.'

Were you specific and clear in stating what you want? Or did your brain trick you and revert to what you don't want?

The theme I've recognised from working with so many of you is that you can tell me straight away what you don't want. When your brain has to access what you do want, often there isn't a file, memory or data there for it to recognise, because as a society we have conditioned it to focus on the pain point.

You could rephrase it to say something like, 'I want to wake up feeling activated, energised and excited. I want a job where I have freedom and choice, creating a load of income while making an impact. I want to work with people I respect and who respect me. I want open and loving relationships with my husband and children, where we can listen to each other and openly discuss our needs, wants, desires and pain points, which creates a happy and harmonious home.'

5. Shake UP

Practice that now and rewrite it in your journal. If you incorporate this self-awareness into your daily life, you're going to have so much more momentum and direction in your life. You're going to have more space to shift, change, grow and learn from your past experiences, instead of getting stuck in old patterns and old ways that are un-resourceful, leading to a cycle of 'never enough'.

Your subconscious mind doesn't recognise negative instructions. For example, if I say, 'Don't think of a big, green elephant – whatever you do, get a big green elephant out of your brain, stop thinking about a big green elephant,' what are you thinking about? Let me guess, I bet you're thinking about a big, green elephant, right? The subconscious mind doesn't recognise 'don't', 'no' or 'stop'. It only hears the command. If you say, 'I don't want to feel tired,' your brain hears 'tired' and looks for data, filters and feedback to give you more 'tired'. I'm certain most of you would prefer to feel 'activated' and 'energised'.

Having this awareness and igniting these neurones that have been lying dormant in your brain will also deepen your bond with yourself.

When you know who you are and what you want (separate from the tangible material things in life), and you declare it in a positive present statement, it gives permission to the universe and spirit to help establish interactions, experiences, relationships and circumstances for you. This provides you with the opportunity and choice to develop, mould and design your life.

The next question I would like you to write in your diary is, 'Who am I?' Before I was asked this question by my mentor, the answer was easy, it sounded something like this– I am a mum of two, thirty-eight years old, a wife, sister and entrepreneur, I am a life coach, personal trainer, athlete, friend ...

However, those are the things I 'do', not who I am.

Get your pen, write, 'Who am I?' then spend some time exploring what comes up for you. I am energy, I am light, I am love.

Evolving family units

Living in the twenty-first century has seen some very chaotic and drastic adaptations to the family unit. With increasing demands and pressure from society, we have created a culture of More and Doing.

Husbands and fathers work more than ever, in FIFO roles or endless hours at office jobs, and are being separated from the family unit. Mothers are left at home to raise the family and often enter back into the workforce to help 'keep up' financially. Many of us are living a life we've been tricked into – overextending ourselves financially, energetically and physically.

To adapt to these changes as a collective, women have evolved to live predominately in 'masculine energy'. Masculine energy is protective, providing, structured, strategic and makes logical sense. Feminine energy is intuitive, flowing, expressive and cyclic. Men and woman can flow in and out of both energies and it's like a delicate dance of direct energy and receiving energy. However, as women we are naturally drawn to being 'feminine' most of the time – and likewise, for males to naturally be in their 'masculine' energy.

Because of the culture and what we have created as a collective, there has been a massive shift; to survive, many woman have adapted into operating mainly from their masculine energy. This plays havoc in relationships, as it creates an imbalance and disconnection from your whole self (and therefore your partner).

5. Shake UP

For me it's a double whammy as I have a FIFO husband, and I'm an entrepreneur and running a business that also calls for oodles of dude energy. I recognised early in our relationship the shift of how I felt as my husband would come and go. It was magnified when we had children and I was so immersed in protection energy.

This is something that we can revisit and adapt accordingly as you feel the need. When you're in business, there are important times when you need to be in masculine mode; when you need the container, framework, schedules, timelines and direction. However, as women, it's our power point to be in our feminine, nurturing, soft, flowing, expressive energy, connected into our intuition.

When you can master the delicate dance of feminine and masculine within the self, it will trickle out and create a positive transformation in your relationship. Where in your current life can you adapt, shift and change what you're currently thinking or feeling to get more awareness around this?

This topic was a game changer for me; when I discovered and danced with the concept, it helped me gain clarity and alignment. There is a time and a place for both, but it's about what best serves you in that moment. It's a beautiful cycle of adapting, opening, flowing and investigating.

I can guarantee that this will open up huge possibilities for your business, your personal life, your relationships, your career and your finances. Sometimes it feels like a really hard slog, because every moment of every day I'm curious. I have to ask myself the questions, drop into the present moment and watch how my behaviour unfolds. Sometimes it gets tiring, but mostly I'm just grateful that I have this awareness – and I've built a team of people around me to help open me up to other ways of living and creating the life I deserve, instead of just reacting to what I've been taught.

Speaking about 'energy' is often a topic that is avoided in business. I'm here as a coach to guide you, mentor you and offer other suggestions and ideas to get you the life that you deserve. I am committed to holding you in your highest power and to weaving in science, spiritually, my insights, my clients experiences and bring you a red hot package of self-discovery and giving you practical, simple strategies and concepts to implement into your life.

We're creative beings and your power and potential are unlimited, particularly when you have the awareness of adaptability, connection and solid, healthy relationships.

It starts with YOU

Integrate the information from this book into your personal life immediately and it will filter through to your business/job and other areas of your life. If you're in a position where you manage other humans, share these insights with them so they can also kickstart the fire in their belly. If you're a parent, share it with your partner and children to enrich their life.

The change starts with YOU. Right now in this moment. Now that you've learnt this, you can't unlearn it. It is now your duty to commit to the change within and open the floodgates of conscious circulation. Imagine with all your senses the ripple effect surging into society with certainty and positive purpose. When you look within and change your own habits, ideas and expectations, commit to awareness and embrace your ability to adapt within ourselves, then we filter this into our business, relationships, into our career.

5. Shake UP

It's been said that the most adaptable species will always survive – so, as humans, we need to adapt to survive. Intuitively, it's something that we all want to do, but because of our ego and outside influence and the way society's been set up, we're kept in a regular routine, a fear-based autopilot state. I'm often met with a lot of resistance when I offer the information and message I have conveyed in this book. Society has some of us in a zombie-like state, just plodding through the days. Consuming.

It's not my role to tell you where to shine the magnifying glass in your life; it's for you to examine your own life and pick what's working and what's not, what feels good and what doesn't. All it may take is a few little tweaks to redirect your focus, language and mindset. I believe with support and belief, you can get more of what you want in life.

I'd like to invite you right now to walk up to a mirror and look deep into your eyes. Down past the black bits, deep down into your own soul.

I remember my first experience of doing this and it was heart-breaking. I couldn't even look into my own eyes; I was distracted by the 'pimples' on my face, the double chin and my crooked eyebrows. I know now that it was all a figment of my imagination and a distraction from connecting with myself, because it was too painful.

When I finally had the courage to look deep into my heart, I was surprised by how I felt. You will have your own experience with this; mine was pure and potent resistance. So dark, uncertain and even hateful. It saddens me to my core that some of you doing this now will feel the same. I looked into my eyes – there was nothing that I could say I liked about myself.

I was at a point where I was willing to do anything to feel better. Regardless of the questioning, resistance and pain, I started looking in the mirror every single morning and saying, 'Diane, I love you, I really, really love you.' I would then sit and observe the feelings, thoughts and emotions which came up with that.

For me, it was resistance. A little voice in my head saying, 'You're lying. You're not worth anything, how dare you say that to yourself?' I had a full body experience and could feel my body tensing up; I felt sick to my stomach and it really surprised me how painful that was for me.

It took me a few weeks, but having been at a point in my life where I couldn't get any lower, I was willing to try anything.

Exercise

Every morning upon waking, walk straight to the mirror, look deep down into your own eyes and say, '(Insert your name here), I love you, I really, really love you.' Observe and listen to that voice – see what it tells you. And report back; I want to hear feedback on how something so simple can completely change your life. Write your feelings into your journal.

Do you tell your mum and dad that you love them? Do you ever pick up your puppy and rub their tummy and say, 'You're such a cutie, I love you, you're so adorable, what can I do to make you happy today?' And if you have children, do you ever tell them, 'I love you'?

So if we tell all the other important people in our life that we love them, and we declare our love for them, then why not do it for the most important person in the world?

Who is the most important person in the world to you? Who is that one person who is there from the moment you're born, every single second, every single day till you die? It's not your mum or your dad or your children or your puppy ... you got it, it's you! So if you can tell your mum or dad or kids or animals that you love them, and show them that, then do it for the most important person in the world – YOU!

> **Essential Oil: Peppermint, Oil of the Buoyant Heart**
>
> One drop into the palm of your hands and inhale.

6. Climb UP

Conquer Mt Washing

I put a post up on social media a few years ago and it was a photo of my mountain of washing, piled up like Mt Everest on the couch. The caption read, 'I told myself, "I'm not going to bed until it's done." Goodnight, it's still on the couch and the world keeps spinning ... and I'll sleep well. I dare you to try it. It doesn't freaking matter.'

Believe it or not, that post had one of the highest engagements (interaction and comments). A boring photo of my clean laundry waiting on the couch. Why? Because it's something every. Single. One of us battle with every day.

Obviously I'm using my washing as a metaphor for the daily housekeeping chores and all that comes with them. You know them well, I don't need to list them for you.

I noticed a conversation on repeat in my internal dialogue – it would play several times a day. 'I really need to get that washing done, there's the washing it's still there. I'll do that after I ...' Every time I walked past Mt Washing, my mind would spin into a flurry of 'should do', 'haven't done yet' dialogue which, although only slight, left me feeling constantly overwhelmed, like I ALWAYS had something to do and I could never go to bed at night feeling complete closure of the day. I didn't think I was 'stressing about it', but by 11 pm on the fourth day when it still sat there waiting (and multiplying) I realised how much internal space it was taking in my mind.

Something had to change. Either I had to get it away immediately or I had to let it go. Really let it go. 'Making time' to put it away would not have changed the pattern in my head. So I decided to break my pattern and make a longer lasting change.

I became acutely aware of my feelings and totally reframed my thoughts, rewiring my subconscious to feel differently about Mt Washing. I wondered to myself, 'When you're lying on your death bed or living within the pivotal moments when something goes horrifically wrong or right in your life, are you going to care whether the washing is done or not?' My answer: a BIG FAT NO.

I now look at Mt Washing with gratitude as the array of colours and textures pile up from, then diminish back to flat ground, from week to week. It means we have clean clothes to wear; it means we have a washing machine to clean them. Folding them each week, I infuse a smile or a little bit of love into the fabric so when my husband, children and myself open our drawers to put on our clothes each morning, an energetic smile sweeps up from the drawer or cupboard and is carried through the day to many others.

6. Climb UP

Folding and hanging is a time of relaxation and meditation, when my mind is quiet and I can focus on what I'm doing. My children now 'help' with the folding, which means we're spending time together as a family and enjoying doing something for each other.

People on their death bed usually wish that they'd spent more time with their family, instead of being at work or getting the washing done or keeping the house clean.

I invite you TODAY to open up a clear communication with the part of your brain that tells you to be a good housewife, you have to have the washing done, the house clean, beds made, blah blah blah. Break your own rules and see how empowering it is.

The washing will always get done eventually – and if it doesn't, ask yourself, 'What's the worst that can happen? What is the worst that will happen if my washing is not done?'

When I've asked clients this, they respond with the fear of somebody coming over and seeing the washing on the couch: 'They're going to judge or criticise or say I'm a terrible mum!'

In my experience, they're going to have a giggle and say, 'My washing is on the couch too,' or, 'I have a spare room that I chuck all my laundry in. Would you like a hand to sort it?'

Do you ever go to somebody's house, see washing on the couch and think, 'Oh, they must be a terrible mum, what a slob'? I'm guessing NOT. Alternatively, if you do think that and you can hear your own judgement and criticism surging through your mind, perhaps it's time to reassess your values and what matters to YOU. What we think and what we portray onto others is actually how we feel about ourselves.

Hear this: regardless of whether your house is clean, washing done, beds made ... it has no indication on what sort of mother, wife or entrepreneur you are.

Free yourself from being perfect and ask more resourceful questions. Change the meaning you give it and FREE yourself from the undue guilt, burden and pressure many of us put onto ourselves. The more freedom and space you have in your head, the more energy you'll have to put towards the things that matter in life: your health, family and conscious business!

In conclusion, I can almost guarantee if you come to visit me to play, share a meal, have a coffee or to attend an event at my home ... there will probably be some form of Mt Washing somewhere in my house. Don't judge me; just love me and share a knowing smile that we're all going through a similar experience. Sometimes she erupts and sometimes she lays dormant, but whatever the day, I'm grateful for this awareness to enjoy her instead of despise her.

Essential Oil – Lemon Oil

Diffuse for an uplifting and crisp aroma.

7. Loved UP

Unlocking Connection

There's an enormous amount of books out on the market that address business relationships. Therefore, I am not going to repeat what has already been written many times over. Let's spend our time together digging deeper and exploring some of your fundamental relationships that create a foothold and foundation for personal momentum and growth.

Fundamental relationships

The relationship that matters the most is the connection and relationship you have with yourself; life hinges from that. If you're frustrated, dishonest, unreliable, degrading and scattered within yourself, you will most likely find outside relationships mirror that.

Other relationships that are high on the authenticity scale and non-negotiable for me are the connections with my children, family network and community. I am immensely grateful for both my immediate and my extended family. None of my achievements to date would have felt as fulfilling without them there to share it with.

Exercise

Take a moment now to contemplate your personal relationships. Draw a straight line horizontally across a blank page in your journal. Write a 1 on the left and 10 on the right. On a scale from 1–10, 10 being the best it can be and 1 being terrible, mark with a BIG LOVE HEART where your relationship with yourself lies on that scale. Then start to add all the important people, bonds and relationships onto that line.

When you've finished, you'll see where you can focus your awareness, energy and commitment to create well adjusted, balanced, harmonious relationships.

> 'The quality of your life is in direct proportion to the quality of your relationships.'
>
> Tony Robbins

Some of you reading this book will have a life partner and children, others might be on a journey of finding one, and there may be some of you who have no intention of finding love. But the common thread that weaves us all together is that we are all human, and humans require connection for happiness. If it's not your partner or children you can relate to through this chapter, relate it to any close relationships that are outside your work environment.

7. Loved UP

Have you ever had the experience where you've kicked some serious butt in business or sport (or something else that you're passionate about) and you're flying high, only to come home to an empty house with no one to share it with? There is a void and longing for somebody to share it with.

What do you do when something amazing happens? When you get a phone call that you got the job? If that boy rings you up to ask you on a date, or you just won a luxury cruise, or when you find out you're pregnant with your first child – what do you do?

Most people call a friend or family member. What do you do if you have really bad or sad news? Most people will call a friend or family member.

There are several reasons you need a safe and secure network of family and supportive relationships when you're rising in your business and life.

Firstly, the framework of supportive relationships helps you feel secure. Sometimes this will be your family members, but if it's not then you need to find a community of like-minded people to share yourself with. It helps you set a structure to unpack your feelings – to communicate your desires, needs, wants and pain points. It gives you space to verbalise those things to a loving and encouraging support network, which can help gain clarity around emotionally triggering experiences.

Celebrate and validate

One thing that is regularly underestimated is the power of 'Validation and Celebration'. It's so important to celebrate the small wins. If you've got no one to share that feeling and energy with, it can be a really lonely and empty feeling. Likewise, when you celebrate and validate with a friend or team of people, the high energy and frequency emanates outwards with electric force.

When I succeed in business or in sport or anywhere in life, it's not just me. Although I might be the face on the front cover or standing on the podium, there has always been a team of people behind me. In my younger years it was my parents, coach, physio; today it's still my parents but also my husband, parents-in-law, brothers, sisters, friends, extended family and followers.

Family, business and life is TEAMWORK

I am one of four children, so we all had to take turns doing chores: helping with the dishes, washing and folding. At the age of sixteen, I learnt a very important lesson about 'teamwork'. Mum and Dad were out one night and it was my turn to do the dishes. I didn't finish my homework until 10 pm, and I still had to make my lunch and iron my uniform – it was about 11 pm before I fell into bed. I had been up at 4 am and needed to get up at 4 am the following morning for intensive training ... I didn't wash the dishes, thinking, 'Dad will do it for me.'

At midnight Dad woke me up, guided me out to the sink and said, 'Wash the dishes, we are a team and it's your turn. You don't get out of it because you are tired, because I'm tired too.' Being a parent myself, I now know how hard that must have been for him to see me in pure exhaustion, but it instilled into me the importance of my place in the team.

A conversation my husband and I have regularly with our children is that we are a team. It's a team effort and we require all members to participate together for a certain outcome. We all have different roles; we're very clear about those roles and we sit down and discuss them often.

I've met many entrepreneurs who work so hard and put so much effort and energy into their business … to go home only to feel lonely. Sometimes they'll stay at work really late to dull the pain of going home to nobody, or to avoid someone at home.

If you find yourself in this cycle, it's possible a lot of your energy is going into patching up that relationship and dealing with that, instead of building and growing momentum in your business.

I'd like to make a disclaimer here: although I know this stuff, I'm being brave and bold in sharing it with you. I don't always do it myself and I need constant reminders from the people close to me to put this into constant practice.

The key is to have awareness and honesty in your relationships. Be open to setting clear boundaries and having the tricky conversations.

Choose presence

Being present is critical in cultivating these nourishing relationships. Make a choice and be there. In the world of social media, it's so easy to be distracted momentarily by the phone dinging, ringing, vibrating or flashing. This awareness changed my life.

Children need at least up to seven minutes of one-on-one time: looking them in the eye, down on their level, doing something that they want to do. I know on the days that I sit with my children and give them my full attention for several minutes throughout the day, they are so much more fulfilled, independent and content within themselves.

Take a moment to reflect on the first interaction with your children, partner or business colleges in the morning. Just like the exercise on mirror work (see chapter 5) and the relationship with yourself, shine some light on your first interaction daily. Does it have a pattern? Are you choosing creative, abundant conversations and connections or just mindlessly plodding through your day?

As in the relationship with yourself, it's those first moments in the day that you cultivate your state and relationship for the day. Think of a time when you've met someone and said hello – and they keep walking by, don't lift their head and grunt you a half-hearted hello. Does that make you feel excited, lively and pumped to connect with them, or does it leave you feeling uncertain, unsure and miserable?

Don't be that person. Enter each interaction with genuine presence, awareness and connection. You may not always feel upbeat and lively but you can still be connected and engaging, regardless of how you're feeling.

Set a solid routine and ritual, regardless of how 'busy' you get.

Set sacred time

My time with my family in the morning is sacred to me, so I set a very solid intention to be home in the morning. I book as much as I can around that time and schedule 'family' time in the morning. We give ourselves plenty of time to get out the door to allow for the tantrums, personality clashes and life lessons along the way.

If you're a shift worker or your schedule doesn't have space for this, sit down right now and schedule daily sacred time with your

7. Loved UP

family. A time and space when you can be present, available and connected with your children and partner.

Another option is bedtime. We always eat dinner together as a family and have space to read a story or two, then lay with the kids and listen to the musings of their day before they fall asleep. It's also a great opportunity to do meditations with them, EFT tapping (to be covered in the final chapter) or listen/discuss what has happened in their day. This time together is also subconsciously teaching them coping strategies, which is priceless in a fast-paced, egotistical world where humans are experiencing so much disconnection.

You may be like me and have some resistance to this. My belief was that the more I did, the better parent and partner I was because I could provide more for my family; the more I did made me feel accomplished and valued. What an empty way to live! Doing, doing, doing … in an attempt to feel full. Living that way is a recipe for disease, disconnection and discontentment.

Pick one thing, do it well

Here is a little story that helped me change my focus. I'm going to share it so you can reflect on your habits and beliefs around 'being productive' or being efficient.

I was running two businesses, Gus was away for work, and I was trying to make lunches, respond to calls, breast feed, clean up, keep myself looking half-decent … basically, I was a raving lunatic most mornings. This was before I had this awareness and opened up to a more practical, fulfilling way of life – I thought I was being really, really efficient by cleaning my teeth, making lunch and closing the fridge door with my foot, all while having the phone up to my ear and responding to people.

I had one child on each leg or in a sling. My cortisol levels were through the roof!

One day I realised as I was racing around the house in total flight or fight mode, I had an 'ah ha' moment. My teeth weren't getting brushed properly and I was making a gigantic mess, leaving toothpaste all over the place and all over my clothes (which meant I had to get changed). I wasn't making the lunches very well, forgetting to pack half the meal. I wasn't talking to the person on the phone properly. I was doing six things at once but none of them were done really well. And because of double handling – having to get changed, driving up to the school to drop the forgotten half of the lunch off – what could have been several ten-minute jobs turned into a half-day ordeal.

Probably the most heartbreaking realisation (all you parent entrepreneurs out there will get this): I was spending enormous amounts of time, effort and energy picking up the pieces of two tiny people who just wanted their mummy to look them in the eye, open the Vegemite for them, give them a hug and do a silly dance in the kitchen. They do not care what you look like, if you have furry teeth for the day, if you have egg and avocado smashed all over your outfit, or how high Mt Washing is.

When you catch yourself trying to do six or seven things at once, I want you to remember this story. Select one thing and give it your full attention until its completion. If it's playing with the children, play with the children. If it's cleaning your teeth, clean your teeth. The way we do one thing is the way we do all things, so spend some time revisiting your habits on the daily tasks.

This concept sounds so simple. Trust me, you'll have to give yourself constant reminders. I started this awareness several years ago and I STILL catch myself in these patterns. When I am at my threshold, I flick back to what I used to do. I regularly catch myself and have to take a deep breath, remind myself of all I've learnt and make a choice and commitment in that moment to be aware of my thoughts, which create my feelings, which lead to my actions. If you can master your thoughts, you'll be able to change your life, business and relationships at a core level.

Exercise

Before you read any further, do yourself a favour and STOP. Set some sacred space with your beloved or accountability partner and have this discussion. Share why you're doing what you're doing; share your vision with all your senses. Just ask them to listen intently. When you're finished, get them to ask, 'And why is this important to you?' Ask this several times until you have goosebumps and tears. When you get to that, you'll know you've hit your WHY.

And then, one simple question: 'What do you want me to remind you of, on the day you decide this is too hard?' Work together to come up with a potent, powerful statement or message to replay to yourself.

Role play this two or three times, until you feel it embedded into your soul.

Communicate clearly

The relationship with your partner, significant other or support person is paramount. Your business will grow and flourish WITH your relationships and awareness. As you cherish your internal world, the outside world will reflect this nourishment, growth and expansion.

Another huge breakthrough for me came when I learnt how to communicate my vision, dreams and mission with my husband. If you don't have a husband, choose a close friend with whom to do this. Ensure they are crystal clear about your dreams, timelines and schedules – and realistically what it's going to take to get there (e.g. time, money, energy, up-levelling as an individual and together, communication). Discuss how you need to be supported by them.

Likewise, LISTEN to what they need from you. Always have an open stream of awareness and communication with a good balance of listening and sharing – absorb their experiences, interpretations and ideas. No matter how busy or heightened it gets, ALWAYS carve out time to come together to support, listen, love and play together. Approach your relationships with a 'what can I give' attitude, instead of 'what can I get'.

Your main support person is an essential part of your journey and success. Gus is my rock. On the days I falter, he believes in me; on the hard days or when I throw my hands up in defeat, he reminds me of my vision. He acts as a steady, unwavering masculine container with such gentleness, love and belief – which generates space for me to drop into my feminine intuition, expression and flow.

I'm also very passionate, direct, driven, determined and disciplined. These are important qualities when starting or running your own business. The lesson for me has been whether these qualities or energies are serving me or keeping me stuck in my ego. The push, the strive, the hustle. There is a time and place for both. The awareness and choice to choose in the moment is the power point.

Have this conversation with your support person so they can also help you determine what is most aligned and authentic to you in that moment.

Even with all this awareness and support, sometimes it still all gets too much. When you're doing the Boss Mum and/or wife, take time to travel, exercise, eat well, or call friends and family. Give yourself the permission to cycle and hibernate when you need to refuel the fire. But if, after a little rest and recalibration, you still want to quit, here are a few rules I stick to.

You can quit, but only on a good day

If you can't get back your mojo, sit with your support person and have them replay the role play of what you said when you first started out with the wind in your wings and the fire in your belly.

Right at the beginning of my business – I remember it like yesterday – Gus and I were sitting at a coffee shop at Merimbula. I had my diary there; we were drawing diagrams and having the conversation of how we could both support each other – and he said to me, 'What do you want me to tell you on the day that you come to me and say this is too big, too hard and you don't want to do it anymore?'

That was such a heart-opening conversation for me. Because in a couple of years' time, when I went to Gus and said, 'This is too hard, I don't think I want to do it any more,' he fed back to me the exact words that I told him.

This meant so much to me that I remember getting tears in my eyes. I took a deep breath, put my head down and bum up, and I carried on with new focus and determination.

Find your 'Gus'

I know I'm one of the lucky ones with such an emotionally aware, supportive life partner. Some of you may not have that, but I wish it for every one of you. I want you all to find your Gus – either in the romantic sense or as an accountability partner, colleague or business partner. It is a team effort and makes the journey so much more expansive and enjoyable.

An observation I've noted many times with my life coaching and business mentoring clients is that women come to me and say, 'My partner doesn't listen to me,' or, 'He doesn't take me seriously, he's not supporting me in my business venture.'

It took me a while to actually verbalise this, because it's quite confronting, but my question to you is, 'How seriously do you take yourself? Are you believing in yourself?'

I know I'm one of the lucky ones, because I did not believe in myself when I started this journey and this venture, and I've met a rock-solid man who has supported me, loved me and believed in me every single step of the way. If you don't feel like you have that yet, we have to create it within you. If you can't do it for yourself, reach out to a friend, a sister, someone – get connected in a tribe of people that see your brilliance and your excellence, that completely believe in you. The power of belief is phenomenal.

If nothing else, contact me, because I believe in you.

If I could believe in myself as much as I believe in you guys, it would be a very different journey for me. Don't hand your power over to your partner. If your partner isn't responding in the way that you want, it could also be that they don't believe in themselves. So it is up to you take back your power and make the change within.

Before we finish up with this chapter, let's touch on professional relationships for a moment. If you're in the corporate world or an entrepreneur who is exposed to lots of different colleagues, customers, supplies, etc. – or it can even be in your personal life – it can be tricky to navigate business relationships. Some industries can be toxic, fostering cultures of less self-aware people, greed, different values, a heightened sense of importance, bitchiness, jealously, criticism and competition. This can lead to bullying, toxic relationships and a downward spiral of your own self-belief and confidence – and therefore, your ability to do your job, connect, and be creative and happy.

I know these situations can be heartbreaking and difficult, as you may feel trapped and powerless. I recommend using tea tree oil immediately, as it is the oil of energetic boundaries. Apply it to your forehead and back of your neck. It will protect you on an energetic level.

Exercise

Next, use this pain point in your life. Instead of asking, 'Why is this happening to me?' ask, 'What can I learn from this?' It's the people who challenge us the most that teach us the most.

Write a list of traits, characteristics or conversations of the other person that annoy you. Then ask yourself, 'Where in my life am I this?' or, 'Where in my life do I do this?' It's a very confronting question because the things that emotionally trigger you about someone else's behaviour can be, on some level, a reflection of the things you don't like about yourself. If you can pinpoint that, then be courageous and dig deep, shine some light and heal it within yourself – then that person (or people) won't have any more emotional charge over you. It cracked my heart right open when I did it; this awareness gave me so much freedom to let go and step into the fullest version of me.

Even the most financially prosperous business is a lonely place without a family or community. I've met too many business people who get to their financial goals but feel emotionally empty, lonely and lost.

A Soulful, successful business to me is one where we cultivate all the important facets: a place of collaboration, connection, creation and expansion. An extension and expression of our Soul Signature – which is who you are at your core, your singular contribution to the world. Your Soul Signature is your spiritual fingerprint, everyone has one – and no one is the same. It is the unique expression of you.

> **Essential Oil – Cedar Wood, the Oil of Community**
>
> A drop into the palm of your hand and inhale.

8. Cashed UP

Money-manifesting Magician

Let's talk about money. People can get uncomfortable when talking about money, as a lot of us tend to have rigid belief systems around finances. Unfortunately, as a society we have many limiting beliefs around what money is, what it means and how much we deserve.

Let's explore your current belief systems around finances and use this chapter as an opportunity to change the way we THINK and to change the way we FEEL, which will change what we DO, which will change what you receive (or don't receive) in your finances.

Exercise

Write in your journal how you feel about money. Do you feel abundant, fun and free – or uptight, constricted and uncertain?

Or perhaps something completely different?

Let's visit your current money story. Answer these questions in your journal.

- What have you been telling yourself about money for all these years?
- What message are you sending *to* money?
- How do you talk about money?
- What sayings do you use regularly?

I was shocked when I first did this exercise to uncover my subconscious identity around money, and where I had blocked and limited my potential of expression and possibility of creative income.

A few of my big ones were:

- 'Money doesn't grow on trees.'
- 'You have to earn things, or work really hard.'
- 'There's not enough money for that.'
- 'Only smart people have money.'
- 'Sacrifice equals abundance.'
- 'I can't afford it.'

Oh my gosh, what was I thinking? Writing this now makes me cringe. If you resonated with any of these, it's time to change your story! While you keep thinking like this, you'll create a destructive cycle of pushing and scarcity.

As a result of those beliefs, I found myself in vicious cycles of striving, pushing, saving, working harder and longer – wondering why there was always a ceiling. I'd push like an Olympic athlete to get there and wonder why I felt drained, fatigued and still not good enough.

I constantly felt like there wasn't enough and I lived in a scarcity mindset, which created more scarcity in all other areas of my life. My money mindset was vibrating at an all-time low.

If you push something, what happens to it? Yes, it gets further away. Let's reframe pushing to being 'pulled' – pulled into the creation and expansion of abundance in all areas of life. Money being one of these.

I was pushing money away; my relationship and awareness with money wasn't attractive, productive or enticing to receiving more. If you put yourself in money's shoes, would you want to go towards someone who didn't really want you or feel deserving of what you had to offer?

Write down what you're thinking and saying about (and to) money. If money was your partner, how would they feel?

What is money? What is your relationship to it – do you love it or hate it? Do you have lots of it, or is it hard to come by? Let this chapter be a catalyst for creating a healthy relationship with the energy society has called MONEY.

Is how you feel on a daily basis different at times in your life when there has been a surplus of money, compared to times in your life there has not been a lot?

Why does it have this power over many of us?

Now that you have awareness around your previous money story and committed to creating a more resourceful one, let's discuss how this might show up for you in business or family life.

If your business isn't performing financially, you notice a drop of income into your family unit. What is the first question or action you commit to? Do you get a flutter of feeling in your tummy? Alternatively, you could be flourishing in these areas but decided to 'step up' and create more of the good stuff. Where do you feel this in your body?

I've noticed a similar sequence in behaviours of entrepreneurs and business owners in these instances. If numbers drop or sales plateau, most of you are primed, planned, strategic and clear on your marketing plans. You know how to increase traction and sales, develop a solid exit strategy and have safety nets in place. I'm not here to tell you how to run your business or family finances, but it will help create clarity on how what you're thinking and feeling is creating the abundance (or lack of) in your life.

Your bank account is a direct reflection of how you feel about yourself and what you think you deserve. This could also be said about your health, relationships and business.

When there's a downturn or plateau in income, or you simply would like to create more income, I'm not saying to sit on a mountaintop humming in bliss and nothing else. A combination of inspired action, recalibrating your cellular vibration around money and changing your relationship to money is key to getting a different outcome.

What's your money story? Spend some time now and revisit the questions I asked earlier. Dig deeper with a new awareness, knowing that what you think on a deeper level will be what is projected into the physical realm.

There is a time and place to take action and engage the systems, strategies, and tangible and measurable processes. It is an important part of the process, but many miss the earlier steps which will make the journey more enjoyable, and a real life example of tuning into your own magical creation powers.

We tend to hand our power over to outside influences. We ask ourselves questions like, 'How can I do more marketing? How can I work more hours? Where can I "save" money? How do I leverage myself to "make more money"?'

Yes, these questions are all relevant and need to be addressed – however, these are only a small component of the things you need to measure and change.

Let's work smarter, not harder. Instead of grinding and pushing, let's change your awareness, understanding and beliefs around money, which will change your vibration. You'll become aware of your values to make the transition into feeling like a money-manifesting magician.

> *'You cannot receive vibrationally something that you're not a vibrational match to.'*
>
> *Abraham Hicks*

If you're listening to the radio and want to listen to punk rock, would you tune into the opera channel? No, you would turn the dial directly to the punk rock channel, turn it up and drown yourself in it. Likewise with our energy waves: if you want to receive abundance, contribution and alignment, would you turn the dial to the scarcity, fear and lack channel, expecting it to play abundance?

What channel are you tuned into? Visualise tuning into more of what you want, right now. Change your dial to match what you want more of. Turn it up!

Imagine, while reading this book, having a surplus of money to contribute to your charity of choice, to help those in need or simply be generous because you can. Add to that visualisation a strong and healthy body, solid and supportive relationships, a career of expression, contribution and love, and a connection to and faith in a higher power and purpose. That feeling is real and will permeate out into the world, creating long-lasting change. This is real wealth.

Every single one of you has this ability right now. Find a way to contribute to something that matters to you. It may be in the dollar value or it could be with your time, assets, talents or energy.

No amount of money can replicate the absolute sense of life, fullness and wealth I feel and radiate from my heart and soul when I witness the sense of homecoming and freedom in friends, family and clients. I get the privilege to work daily with humans and remind them of their power, and to see that moment of connection when the sparkle returns to their eyes and their passions are reignited. They tune back into their power as creative, expressive beings. Their radio station has changed back to love, abundance, freedom and creation. There is no amount of money that can give me that feeling.

Connection and contribution. That's why I wrote this book: I want this for more of you.

Conscious circulation

Conscious circulation of money – and how we spend and invest our resources (time, money, energy) to serve other people and other small businesses – is one of the most empowering, heart-filling, life-altering daily choices you have. Choose wisely. You can help give freedom to another mother or father to stay home with their children, if that's what matters to them, or hire a nanny to go to work if that is what their heart calls for. Let's drop the judgment, criticism and competition and choose to uplift those around us. This is true wealth.

Something that's really shocking to me is that over 3 million people in Australia are living below the poverty line. That means there's 3 million people in Australia, some of whom could be living in your neighbourhood, who can't afford the bare necessities of life. That is heart-breaking to me, so I want to use this book to create an impactful, open awareness and show you how you can focus on connection and relationships, and have the money flow towards you. Not having money in your life can lead you to feeling trapped, frustrated or relying on someone else to pay your wage or give you money; you're left feeling powerless. The more that you feel like this, the more that you create the crappy experiences in your life.

A word of warning: many people think once they hit that magic amount of money, they will be 'happy' – the 'I'll be happy when xyz' syndrome. A surplus of money doesn't create happiness. Don't fall into this trap … I believe money is a vessel or a tool in helping you step into freedom and choice. When you have more, you can give more. There are plenty of financially wealthy people out there who are unhappy.

Wealth to me is abundance, awareness in all areas of my life and the ability, capacity and flexibility to recognise and make changes as I expand and grow as a mum, wife, daughter, sister and businesswoman.

Exercise

If you find yourself in the 'I'll be happy when' syndrome, it can be very unfulfilling and soul-destroying. Visit a memory of when you wanted something so badly – the boyfriend, the car, the job, the body – and you worked so hard to get it, only to get there and find out you still felt a void. I can guarantee most of us would have at least one experience in life where we've felt this.

Now, instead of working vigorously towards it without any more thought, ask yourself, 'What is the feeling I think this 'thing' will give me?' Is it certainty, love, freedom, connection, security?

Tangible assets will not create these things. It starts from within by changing the radio station. As a society we're doing it the wrong way around, aiming to 'get the things' to be happy. We need to create happiness and peace from within – then all the outside things will be an extension or bonus on that.

Once you have clarified the feeling you think 'xyz' will give you, instead of going outside yourself by using money or things to feel that way, go within and change your ideas, beliefs and relationship with yourself.

Intensely focus on the feeling that 'xyz' will bring you, then meditate on that. This will help shift your vibration and your awareness, opening a place of connection and alignment within you.

If you focus on feeling full and connected – and cultivate nurturing relationships with yourself, others and money – the income will follow.

When I first heard some of these possibilities for changing my business and bank balance, I had lots of objections ... and you might find yourself asking questions right now. For example, it sounded totally ridiculous to me how can I magically manifest all this money by simply changing my relationship with it. I had ingrained within myself that I wasn't worth it and I didn't deserve it, until I learnt that money is a vibration and brought together the worlds of science and spirituality.

Science tells us your brain does not know the difference between something vividly imagined with all your senses and a memory. This information changed my life. When you drop into the desire, outcome or moment in your life, you are calling in and adding all your senses to it. Here, a part of your brain called the reticular activity system kicks in. It filters and organises information to find interactions, conversations, experiences and interactions related to anything you continually think about. If you trick your brain into believing you have wealth, then it will find data and ignite neurons to support that. WOW!

There's an NLP strategy known as Timeline Therapy, which I still use a lot in manifestation. It is such a powerful strategy and I offer it in one-on-one coaching sessions, group seminars and online programs.

We are at our most powerful when we bring the best parts of science and strategy together with spirituality and energy.

Are you ready to change your money story, create new beliefs, reignite your passions and receive abundance? Put on that magician hat, turn the radio up, sit back and enjoy the show.

> **Essential Oil – Frankincense and Wild Orange**
>
> A drop of each in your wallet and on your belly button.

9. Stand UP

Perfect Boundaries

Boundaries come on so many levels, but for the purpose of this book let's stay focused and keep it simple, so you can integrate this information with ease and grace. This chapter is about how you can firmly and fairly set and honour important boundaries. This will protect you from overcommitting and feeling pulled from pillar to post, as well as allowing you to start each day purposefully with focused vision and clear intentions.

Setting boundaries

Setting and adhering to my own boundaries (and that of others) is something I've had to work hard on. For so long I resisted any kind of boundaries, schedules or anything that had me feel 'trapped' or 'controlled' (the hippies and disrupters reading this book will know what I mean). Now I know that these are the things that create trust, space, structure and a framework to keep our lives and business in direct harmony and alignment.

Basically, you've got to do what you say you're going to do. You've got to instil from a very early stage a solid framework of trust within your family unit, work colleagues and lifestyle networks.

For a very long time, my pattern showed up in overcommitting and not appreciating or respecting my time. I recognised it in the early days of staring my holistic business. Often my mum would look after the children while I worked. I would say, 'I'll be back in two hours,' and I'd rock back up three or four hours later. Mum didn't mind having them for that long, but because I hadn't been clear and honest, it interfered with her day and plans. I wasn't respecting her boundaries.

I would NEVER rock up two hours late for a customer or client, so why would I do it to one of the most important people in my world?

I justified it to myself because I wasn't because sitting with my feet up in a park having coffee or watching TV; I was out serving people and making connections. Sometimes it's the most important people in our lives who get the raw end of the deal, because at the end of the day we know they'll love us anyway.

Once I realised my pattern (hopefully I've ignited something in you to recognise yours), I changed it immediately. Changing my behaviour, language and conversation with my mum has created so much more freedom and harmony for both of us. It's also strengthened our relationship and understanding of each other.

This interaction also led to me assessing my behaviours and boundaries within my immediate family unit. It wasn't unusual for me to tell Gus I would be home for dinner at 6.30 pm and rock up an hour or two after that, because I got busy or had a meeting go overtime. He never said anything, as he could see the pressure and stress I had already put myself under. It creates an undertone of uncertainty that sits under the surface and chips away at the family unit.

One of the gifts of being an awakened soul is the constant questioning and delving deeper, which in this instance is how I recognised that once again I had been acting in the pattern of not honouring my word.

Now I make a superhuman effort to always do what I say. If say to Gus, 'I'm going to be home for 6.30 for dinner,' I need to make sure I'm home at 6.30. If something does pop up, I make a conscious decision in that moment. If I choose to stay, I call Gus and let him know what is going on. Although it does happen, it is rare. I'm so grateful for this awareness of something I resisted for so long; it really does feel so much better.

It's important that if you tell the kids you're going to be somewhere or do something, you have to follow through; you have to be there when you say you're going to be there.

Communication with yourself, your support people, and your staff and colleagues is paramount. Honour your word; set and keep your boundaries, and respect theirs. If you find yourself pushing boundaries, being late and not keeping your word, then that will be reflected back to you and people will find it hard to take you seriously.

Be clear about your boundaries and what is acceptable. Set a culture of respect, empowering and inspiring people instead of having them rely on you.

Take time off

The last thing that I'll talk about is taking time off. I know a lot of you won't want to hear this, because we're entrepreneurial and we're driven – a lot of us associate getting stuff done with being successful and validated, and getting somewhere in life. It took me a long time to realise that my time off is a part of that process. My time off is to be completely off social media and give myself that time to rejuvenate myself – to have those conversations that, when I'm in my busy cycle, I don't have time to have. It's about filling myself up.

And you know what? It's also taking time off from the family. That's just not for work. I can guarantee that a lot of you female entrepreneurs get time off, but then you spend it doing everything for the family. You need time off for yourself. Maybe get a massage once a week or fortnight.

You need to take that time to self-care and self-nurture, because our children are mimicking our patterns – so if we're working, working, working to feel productive, validated, loved and successful ... then that's what our children will do.

As you all know, our children don't do what we tell them; they do as we do. They duplicate our patterns. Do you want to teach your children to get on the hamster wheel, run the rat race and never take a day off, just because you don't know what to do with your mind on a day off?

That's certainly not what I want to teach my children. I want to teach my children that they are perfect and complete just the way they are. To do a job or create an income by doing something that completely lights them up, that serves people ... something where they have freedom to do the things they want, when they want, while creating a massive impact. That's what I want to teach my kids.

> **Essential Oil – Tea Tree, the Oil of Energetic Boundaries**
>
> Small drop on third eye and behind ears.

10. Guilt DOWN

Eliminate Mother's Guilt

Grab yourself a warm tea or a hot cacao and tuck yourself in, I've saved the best until last.

Mother's guilt can feel like a big black blanket that steals your joy, makes it hard to function and clouds your mind, making usually easy decisions impossible. It can come on in a tsunami of emotions or trickle in, bit by bit. However it shows up, it can be debilitating and have heartbreaking consequences for individuals and families.

We are losing mums and wives to the workforce and families are breaking down, because we haven't been given a realistic expectation of what going back to work with children can look like.

Being a parent is a challenging role – add the pressures and expectations of running your own business or working outside the family unit, and I guarantee that there's been times of utter exhaustion, frustration, anger, uncertainty and the 'G' word: 'GUILT'. It can feel like having your heart ripped from your chest because you feel burdened and responsible for the weight of the world because you're juggling daily, important roles and decisions that impact and shape your life and the lives of others.

We are at an all-time high for mothers returning to work, which is both exhilarating and scary. As a collective, we are so grateful for these opportunities and freedoms our ancestors have fought hard for … however, with light there is naturally a shadow. Mother's guilt is part of the shadow for this renewed freedom and choice.

As a whole, society's expectations are high and often unsustainable, coupled with patterns of overachieving and striving drilled into us from a young age as a metric for feeling worthy and accomplished. Many women are returning to work feeling empty, scattered and pulled from pillar to post.

If you choose to be an entrepreneur or return to the workforce after you have children, it's my intention that you do it on your terms, on your timeline and with what feels good for you. To have a realistic expectation of your resources and energy levels requires you to create your reality.

Be gentle

Mother's guilt can be a very sensitive topic, so it's essential we approach this chapter with gentleness. At any stage if you feel angry or emotional, be gentle with yourself and become your own observer. Take yourself out of your own emotions and watch from the sideline as if you're watching a movie. Get curious about how things could change for you to create something different in your life.

10. Guilt DOWN

I've also left this chapter to the end because it is definitely one of the hardest ones to write; it's something I need to check with myself momentarily and if I don't stay committed to it, I could be washed off my feet at any moment.

> *'The greatest gift you can give to another person is your happiness.'*
>
> *Ester Hicks*

As I write this chapter, we are away on the Gold Coast and I've carved out two hours of time where Gus, my husband, has taken the children out to the beach and ice cream with my mum and grandma so I can have the time to put in the finishing touches. Part of me dearly wants to be at the beach with the kids, but another part of me – driven, focused and determined – has made the commitment to write this book and share my message and vision.

I could sit in front of this computer, typing, feeling an overwhelming burden of want, scarcity and longing – like I've let my kids and family down, because I'm not with them. Or, I can choose gratitude and continue to share with absolute certainty, balance and alignment, knowing that I've made a choice in the moment that feels good.

I allocate sacred time every day when I can be totally present with my kids. I rarely compromise on these times, being morning routine and bedtime.

My kids don't need me there every second of the day; what they do need is a full, aware and connected Mummy who is present when I'm with them – and full and connected when I'm not with them. I don't have to pretend I'm 'happy' all the time, but I need to honour the ups and downs of my life and share them as well.

If you're getting everything that you need on a soul level as a mother or a parent, it's more likely the children and your partner will be getting what they need. We often fall into the trap of 'doing' everything on the outside of ourselves to help our nearest and dearest, feeling empty for our own needs. If your cup is empty and you crash and burn, who will look after your nearest and dearest then?

I've changed my thinking and therefore can sit here on the computer and be totally present and focused in writing this chapter, dispelling any feelings of guilt or inadequacy. This is far better than the options I used to give myself before I had this awareness:

1. go to the beach and feel guilty the whole time I'm there, that I should be writing my book

2. stay, write and feel guilty I should be with the kids.

Sound familiar?

Run your own race

In 2017, I went overseas for the first time without my children. Ross was five and Esme was three. I have international followers and I heard their call to head over to the USA to share my vision and message. So I went to America to host workshops. I also had a dear friend's wedding over there, so I aligned the trip and did both.

I was away for three weeks of kid-free time and it was the very first time I'd left them, particularly for 'work'. Reflecting on these moments and decisions, I recognise many conflicts in my belief systems.

It was a time of huge growth and momentum, and an opportunity to dive deep into the world of mother's guilt.

I was absolutely stunned by the amount of people who asked me:

1. do you miss them?
2. do you feel guilty?

This subconsciously plagued me because even asking these questions set the undertone of an expectation that I should.

When I first left I was overcome by feelings of despair and uncertainty, filling my head with traumatic events that 'could' happen to me (or them) while I was gone. How would they go without me, how would I go without them, ahhhh – it was intense. And then all these people I perceived judging me as a bad mum because I left my kids.

I had a decision to make: I COULD NOT live the next three weeks with this feeling churning in my mind and soul.

Feel the feelings and CHOOSE

Let me share my transition in hope that it can give you some tips to loosen the grips or completely release guilt altogether.

I remember the transition period clear as day: driving out the driveway on the way to the airport, leaving my children for the first time. I felt uncertain scared and worried. A sick feeling consuming my whole being.

As I looked back at them waving, I made a decision to be grateful in that moment instead of feeling scared, worried, or like a bad mum for leaving my kids – I chose to feel gratitude. Grateful that I have the most incredible husband and extended family who are available and excited to share life with our little family.

I was also grateful for the opportunity for the connection between the children and their father and grandparents, which can flourish differently without me there. It shows the children there are other people who can support, encourage and help them when I'm not around. When I go away, it gives them the opportunity to get to know each other without me there. That is important. I think we would all agree that kids are different when their mum is around.

Gratitude was the first decision I had to make. The second decision in that instant was to honour my feelings and let myself be sad. Up until this moment it felt like I'd spent nearly every second of every single day with my children, apart from when I went to the toilet (well, most of the time they're there as well!).

Instead of chastising myself, I chose to be gentle and kind to myself. I gave myself a time limit to feel the icky feelings – I gave myself until the flight to feel sad. I let myself cry. Gus dropped me off at the airport and said, 'Don't be sad.'

I replied, 'It's okay to be sad, it's part of the process.' Feeling sad and scared was a part of the process for me: I accepted and surrendered and took one moment at a time. If I didn't let myself work through it and convinced myself it didn't bother me, it would have caught up with me eventually. Alternatively, I could've remained in sadness the entire three weeks I was away – neither sounded like attractive options to me.

What are you ready for? What are they ready for?

There's another critical consideration with each decision we make in extending the time and space barrier with our children as they grow developmentally: what are they ready for? Each child is different, each parent is different and each situation is different. There's no one simple answer to this.

I encourage you to dive deep and investigate. Trust your intuition as a mother and your connection with your children. I observe my kids before I make decisions that I know are difficult for me as a mother. Every parent's threshold is different, but I feel like it makes it easier for everyone when I tune into what they're developmentally seeking.

Was I going to leave my three month old child for three weeks? No. Some of you might and that's totally fine, but it wasn't for me. I decided when Esme turned three and Ross was five, they didn't need me as much emotionally – that was the right time for me to take this trip. I had opportunities in the past to go away, but I decided not to take them, because it didn't feel right for me … it didn't feel like they were ready, and I wasn't ready to have that distance.

Everybody's different; this is not a criticism of any other parents but for me and my family and my children, that's when I felt comfortable. For some of you it will be at three weeks, or at three months – whatever it is that you decide, as long as you decide it with consciousness, then that's the right answer for you.

So I jumped on the plane and over I went to America. I went to my friend's wedding and I just felt so blessed and so amazing. I was working while I was over there, doing workshops and one-on-one consultations and events, all of which I really, really enjoyed, reminding you of the questions I got asked the most: do you miss your kids? Do you feel guilty?

If I hadn't had the awareness and gone through the above process, the answer would've been a big fat YES for sure.

I had drafted a post for social media about this, and then chickened out on posting, because I was petrified of what people would say and think about me. I was ashamed of my answer, because the belief system I had told me I was a bad mum if I didn't feel guilty. Do you miss your kids? No. Do you feel guilty? NO. Does that make me a bad mum? NO.

If I started to 'miss' the children, I made a decision in that moment to stay focused and present in the conversation, interaction or experience. There was no time or space in my mind for me to miss the kids.

If you're experiencing this – that pull between work, children and your own needs – then first of all, you've got to sit down and get really clear about what their ages are and what's comfortable for you. You've got to direct it. Don't just react; don't just look at your finances and say, 'Oh I need to go back to work now, because that's just the way it is.' I used to think like that as well but it's not the way, because no amount of money can buy back the time with your family and loved ones. I promise you that.

Dance your best dance

I've made direct choices to take other avenues in life other than being a mum, so on top of that I'm obviously a wife, an advocate and a guest speaker – I run retreats and my life can get very full. But it's a moment-by-moment dance of questioning how I'm feeling, how the kids are feeling and what I need to do in the moment to feel the fullest and the most aligned.

If you take that time to set those foundational, fundamental things, the rest of life is going to be so much easier.

And don't throw your hands up in the air if your kids are older; I've worked with so many women in my business mentoring who tell me that they feel terrible because they spent so much time at work. But let me tell you right now: whatever your decisions have been in the past, it was because you thought they were the best choices. Even if you don't feel like that now in the pit of your stomach, move forward knowing that at the moment you made those decisions, you thought it was for the best.

So, fast forwarding into the spot where you are now, if you're having those icky feelings, just honour them; let them go to the side. Know what you did to get there and do something different.

Fit your own oxygen mask first

Now you're going to set foundations and get really deep into what you need to feel full – how you need to show up as a mum or as a wife. Not for everybody else, but for you. I said it earlier and I'm going to say it again: when you're happy and aligned and balanced as a mother on a soul level, fitting your own oxygen mask first, it's more likely that your children and your husband are going to be happy. If you're coming up feeling drained, run down, frustrated and angry, then that is going to transfer onto them and they will pattern that.

I think in that instant of me going overseas for three weeks, because I had the foundations set and I made a conscious choice, I dropped into the way that I felt and what I was comfortable with. It was a little bit of a stretch, yes, because it was different, but that's what life's about to me. That's the foundation: how do I feel about that? Are they ready?

It doesn't mean it's not going to be hard; sometimes it's hard for you and sometimes it's hard for them. But if you've set that foundation, done the work and made that decision, then honour that decision and move forward.

You can change your mind

Do you know what the real beauty of this is? If at any moment in time I feel like something shifts or changes in my life (or my children's life or my husband's life), I can make a different decision. If I'd gone to America and I didn't feel good about it, or my intuition told me I needed to be home, do you know what the most powerful thing is? I have the decision to change my mind. I can pack up and come home.

The moment I realised that, it gave me so much freedom. I want to offer that to you as a strategy as well. If you're really busy at work (or whatever you're doing) and it's not working for you, you have the power to change it. You are the creator of your own life.

I'm set up so that I cycle things. I feel into my kids' ages and how much they need me. Now they're a little bit older – Ross is six and Esme is four – so I go away for a little bit longer and a little bit more often. But moment by moment, I check into how I'm feeling, what I've got on right in that moment and coming up, and I cycle it. I might be away for seven days at different courses, seminars, public speaking gigs and retreats, but in my head, I know after that seven days that I have allocated

10. Guilt DOWN

3–4 days (or 5–6, however many I decide) to being completely, wholly and solely with the kids. There for pickups, there for bedtimes, there for everything.

Set sacred space

There's another thing I do at a foundational level ... and ladies, this is not hard, but it's really important and it's easy to skip, because in the moment it doesn't feel like it's got that much weight to it.

Every single morning that I'm home, my children know that they get my undivided attention, depending on what time we wake up (we don't wake up to an alarm). I feel blessed and grateful that I get to wake up to my body clock and then the kids come in and lay with me.

Recently I've started getting up early and sitting by myself first ... and as they trickle out, they come and sit with me with no devices: no TV, no iPhones, nothing. We just sit. Sometimes we talk but we may just sit for a good 30 minutes, sometimes up to an hour; we just hang out and talk about what they want to talk about.

I'd like to invite you now to pick one time every single day that is sacred for you and your family. I feel like I've gotten to a point now where sometimes I say yes to something happening during the morning ... but I check in and notice how I'm feeling. I notice how the kids are feeling and I look at what I've had on, then what I've got coming up as well, before I'll say yes to anything in the morning.

Visit your life and feel what works for you; spend that time with the important people in your life. For the purpose of this book, it's mainly children – I feel like that's where we're getting pulled apart in one direction – and our husbands as well. So guys, it's not just about the kids; it's about how you feel and how you show up as a wife. You need to set that sacred time.

Don't just 'get home' – BE HOME

Regardless of how busy I've been throughout the day or how much I've had on throughout the day, I'm so lucky because Gus has really stepped up in helping take care of the family, making dinner and keeping the house running, so I can walk in, I hug everybody and we can sit down and eat our meal together.

I'll always put them to bed and lay with them for 10–30 minutes – or up to an hour if it's left to Esme's decision. She'd have me lay there with her all night. That's an internal struggle that I go through every night; the thought in my head is, 'Oh, 10–15 minutes, because I've got so much work to do and calls on after I put her to sleep.' I lay with her 10–15 minutes and my next thought is, 'She's only young once, she wants me to lay with her until she falls asleep' – and it can take her up to an hour or more to fall asleep.

I can't give you a single answer, because every single night is different. If I drop out of my head and into my heart and I connect with her, I know when she needs me there and I know when she's testing for boundaries.

The key is to be in the moment. That means sometimes I've got to cancel calls, which I don't like to do. But having children and having a family – something I value so much – has taught me that I've just got to ask myself what's most important in that moment. Most of the time, it's laying with her, but not all the time. That's something that you've just got to decide in the moment.

Speak their love language

There are five different love languages; we each give and receive love differently. Knowing your own language and that of each family member is critical in cultivating healthy and full relationships, which helps eliminate guilt.

1. Words of affirmation
2. Quality time
3. Gifts
4. Physical touch
5. Acts of service

Ross loves to do things together– and if you've watched my social media, you'll know this, he's quite a clever little button – he absolutely adores making stuff. So, in the mornings, my time with him is usually spent drawing or making some paper planes or Lego models; that's far beyond my capacity but he's looking up at me with these adoring eyes, wanting me to help. It challenges me every morning! It's just not my thing!

When Gus is home, the boys spend hours tinkering and building stuff together.

Esme enjoys colouring and playing shops. Every morning she pretends she is the owner of a crystal and essential oil shop and we have the exact same conversation. Every morning she lights up like it's the first time she's heard it! I connect differently with each of the children and spend time with each of them, speaking in their love language.

I want to be open, honest and raw with this book. It's no use pretending everything's perfect and fine and 'Brady Bunch' all the time in our house, because it's certainly not. I'm a mum and a wife, an entrepreneur doing the best that I can every single day. Some days it works, some days it doesn't work.

If you want to be and do all those amazing things and have the same highs and lows – but the ability and the capacity to recognise where you're at, where you want to be and how to close that gap between the two – then this is the journey for you.

Sacrifice

Before I finish up, I want to touch on sacrifice. I always believed that sacrifice was a key element to success. For example, in my finances: instead of creating more, I would sacrifice. I would sit and watch everyone else drink coffee or eat dinner and 'save my money.' In my relationships, instead of asking for more, I would sacrifice time and what mattered to me. To get more or do more, I would sacrifice things.

For a long time I also thought being a good parent or wife meant I had to sacrifice the things that matter to me. Yes, there is definitely an element of putting someone else's needs ahead of your own. But when you can do that with conscious connection, it's a very different feeling when it comes from an abundant conscious mindset compared to a lack or scarcity mindset.

There are several basic human needs – I'm not going to go into them in this book. But as long as you're getting most of yours met, then you're going to be able to help your children get most of theirs met.

10. Guilt DOWN

What a lot of us do is go outside of ourselves; we see or feel what we think our partners and our children need, and then we go about busily trying to provide that for them. The best thing that we can do as a mother is be aware of what our needs are and get those met, because then that leaves us completely full, aligned and able to help them work out what their needs are ... and show them how to get it for themselves.

Otherwise, you'll find yourself being the martyr, doing everything for everyone for the rest of their lives. You'll wake up feeling exhausted and on autopilot – and that is not what I want for you.

This book is about waking up the giant within; it's about switching off the autopilot and creating more of what you want, while saying no to the things that you don't want. You deserve this; you are good enough for this. And if I – a shy, timid little girl from Ipswich – can get up in front of thousands of people and share this message, if I can write a book and make this happen with all of your support, then I fully believe that each and every single one of you can as well.

If you've purchased this book there's a reason for it, so sit in silence by yourself and tune in – connect to who you really are. What do you really want in life? Let's start taking some steps to get there.

Society has put so many layers on top of what we really want that we've forgotten. So, this is about remembering – this is about having a homecoming and saying, 'I don't want my life to be that way anymore. This is what I want from now on.'

When we work together as a tribe, we get those fundamentals in place. It's just like a big, beautiful snowball that maintains momentum and just keeps expanding. So, let's do that.

Rise UP

I want you to put this book somewhere you can see it regularly – and every single time you look at it, you can get a little trigger of certainty and clarity, and a reminder about what you're here for and how you could feel every day if you let yourself.

> **Essential Oil – Forgive**
>
> Rub on your feet and heart before bed.

11. Power UP

Three Steps to Lift Off

Step 1 – Change up passwords

There are so many of us at work or logging onto internet banking for the thousandth time, entering our password into the computer. Passwords of pet names, or the street that we used to live in, or our mother's maiden name, or some random name. Reflecting back on what you've read so far about internal dialogue, ask yourself now what entering those names ten times a day is creating for you.

I want you to go in right now and change every single password to a word or a state which you desire. We can emotionally anchor that state, so every time you type it in, you get a little feeling of that state.

I'm not going to tell you mine, because you'll know all my passwords, but here's some examples.

'Love123456': every time you type that into the computer you're going to get a trigger of it.

'Joy': add the numbers if you want, '111', means you're on track – your angels are here, so every time you enter 'joy' you feel joy.

If you're going through something that requires a lot of courage at the moment, type in 'courage' and then pick a number that means something to you, such as '888' for the infinity symbol. If you're ready for a relationship, use that. If you're expanding in your career, write that one word that creates the feeling you desire in your passwords.

I don't want to give you more things to do, but what I do want is to help you visit your current patterns, all day, every day – and how we can shift and change them to create your life, instead of reacting to it.

Give me feedback (you don't have to tell me your passwords) and share this with your friends. It's something so simple that will make such a huge difference.

Step 2 – Tap up with EFT tapping and anchoring

EFT tapping has been one of the single most easy and effective ways I've been able to move through challenges in my life, to break old belief patters and behaviours. I was so lucky to learn the technique as a fifteen year old girl. I was so lost, lonely and depressed when I saw a very dear friend who is also a holistic health worker. She taught me the technique of EFT tapping.

11. Power UP

I had no idea of how it worked, and I didn't really care. I was at such a low point that I didn't ask any questions; I trusted with full faith because I figured it couldn't get any worse and I was willing to try anything.

When I plunged back into the darkness, I would just tap, tap, tap. As I got more awareness around how I was feeling, I would pinpoint icky feelings of guilt, resentment, loneliness, isolation, grief – if anything came up, I would simply tap it away.

As I started to move through grief and trauma, and tackle old patterns of depression and helplessness, I slowly started to unfurl my wings and break out of the cocoon. EFT tapping is something I'm ultra-passionate about, as it's an easy, effective and accessible way to create change at a deep level. As humans, we complicate things – EFT tapping simplifies everything. Still to this day I tap daily, sometimes several times a day.

I'm not going to go into the scientific explanation in this book – there are loads of textbooks and podcasts that can explain it.

If you're reading this book and have made it all the way to these last chapters, then my guess is you've enjoyed sharing with me and trust the process. You believe in me and my message, so I invite you to trust this process. To trust in me and all the thousands of women and men I've worked with, who have welcomed EFT tapping with open arms.

It's useful if you have an un-resourceful state or pattern appearing regularly – for example, fear, anxiety, depression or overwhelm. You might be going into a business meeting or have a proposal that you've got to organise, but you have those fluttery feelings. Likewise, it could be in your home life with the kids behaving in a certain way, or your husband being at work, and you feel overburdened. Whatever it is for you, spend a moment to pinpoint it. Let's practise using that state or feeling.

We will use the words 'although I feel anxious'. Repeat these words while tapping on certain parts of your body:

> 'Even though I feel anxious, I deeply and profoundly accept myself.'

Look up the website, **www.dianemckendrick.com**, to get your FREE 'how to' video.

Whenever I had those fears arise, feeling them in my stomach or my chest, my breath shortens and my movements hasten. I start behaving in a way that isn't healthy for me. It takes commitment to notice how you're feeling each moment of each day, as un-resourceful states can sneak up on you. You can be in a fit of rage or flurry or anxiety before you brain even registers. Choose this new relationship with yourself and the very moment you recognise these feelings, START TO TAP.

> 'Even though I feel (insert your word here), I deeply and profoundly accept myself.'

I have found it ultra-useful when driving through traffic and I feel myself getting frustrated at other drivers ... I start my tapping.

Even though I feel frustrated, I deeply and profoundly accept myself. I also use this time in the car to set my state for the day. I'll do my tapping in there, particularly if I'm going to an important appointment, a big meeting or a media stint. Or when I'm hosting an event with a lot of people and I'm feeling a bit jittery and nervous, I'll do my tapping all the way there. Use the time in the car or transit to do your tapping.

Thankfully, EFT tapping is very discrete. You can effectively tap in a group of people, on stage, or while in a meeting. While I'm speaking in front of hundreds of people, if I feel the nerves rise, I'll simply tap my thumb onto my little finger; nobody can see and it has the same result. Likewise, if I'm in a meeting with the bank or the accountant, which tended to make me nervous in the past, I just tap on the side of my head like I'm thinking, and I can feel that filter through my body.

Please don't underestimate the power of EFT tapping. I know I haven't given you a technical background or a scientific explanation of how this works, and I know most humans want the nuts and bolts – please trust and have your own experiment with it.

EFT tapping continues to assist me to stay in the states that are resourceful to me, and to land me into my body with awareness of what my thoughts and feelings are creating in my reality.

If you decide you'd like to work with me one-on-one or do one of my online courses, there will almost always be an element of EFT tapping in there.

Lots of practitioners have a different style or a different way that they implement tapping. I recommend following the video on our website to get started.

There's also 90-day online courses that take you through EFT tapping every single day – tapping on different beliefs, systems and fears that are holding us stuck and holding us back.

What are your dreams and aspirations? Would you like to write a book? Would you like to get up and present in front of hundreds of people? Or perhaps you're more of a computer person and you want to start an online program? Get healthy, start a family, meet the person of your dreams – the opportunities are endless and the only thing that will stop you is YOU.

Start EFT tapping now and release blockages that stop you from moving forward.

I've also started tapping with my children Ross and Esme. Quite often, as he goes to bed at night, Ross will ask me to do his tapping for him.

Everything I offer in this book can also be done with your children. Fit your own oxygen mask first and then, with time and consistency, it will filter through to your partners, friends, family and colleagues.

Now I've shared my secret; if you see me at an event gently tapping my forehead, you'll know what I'm doing. I've kept it a secret for far too long – I was petrified of what people would think. I didn't want people to think I was 'strange'. It's time to totally own it and I'm so thrilled to be able to share it with you.

Another awesome technique I'd love to include here is anchoring. Our life is a series of triggers. Things happen in your life; they trigger you into a certain state and then you get the outcome. But what's happened in the past is that we haven't had conscious triggers. As a child we made our truth from everything we've been told, because we don't have a filter. The ideas, beliefs and opinions of adults, siblings, teachers and friends have become your truth.

If you've been through traumatic experiences as a young child, when you hear a certain word or hear a loud noise, it will trigger you into a certain state. The power of anchoring is that we can regain control and direction. Let's let go of what we don't want and consciously choose more of what we do want in our life.

It's time to visit our triggers and set them consciously, to create our life and stop reacting to it.

What do you think when you're driving and see a red light? Write it in your journal. What do you think when you hear the phone ring? Start to investigate how you feel in different areas of your life. Then, focus on what some of your triggers could be. Are they setting you up for success or keeping you in your own prison?

I would like to share an example (there is many) of when I used anchoring to help solidify a resourceful state, rather than reacting to 'how I thought I felt'.

Esme, my daughter, was six weeks old and, as most, would wake up numerous times every night. At the time I was a personal trainer in my boutique home gym, a dream come true. I trained a beautiful pod of amazing women for several years. Through that period, Esme wasn't sleeping much (which meant I wasn't sleeping much).

I had up to ten clients a day; there were definitely times that I would get tired. Just the thought of a restless night's sleep and full day's work was enough of a trigger to convince me I felt tired!

I was fully booked, back to back, with up to ten clients a day. I allocated time in-between to eat, train and breastfeed Esme. I would wear her in a sling most of the time, unless my dear mum was there to help out (Which, many days, she was!).

There were times I was physically, emotionally and mentally exhausted. These beautiful women were all as important as each other, so I had to give as much love, energy and attention to the first person in the morning as that last person at 7 pm. The only way that I could do that is to trigger energy and alertness, instead of slipping down into being really tired.

Who wants to know how I did this? Who could do with an injection each day (or a few times a day) of real, raw, potent energy?

In a quiet time on my own, I would hold onto my left earlobe and remember a time when I felt completely activated, energised, focused and connected. As I hit the peak of that state in my memory, I would squeeze lightly on my ear and anchor that feeling in there. Repeat it several times to anchor it in.

Even today as I write this book and I press onto my left earlobe, I can feel that joy, love and energy just pulsating through my body. This is absolutely magic to help create the state that you want to be resourceful – to get more of the things that you want.

There are so many ways you could use this technique. Spend some time thinking now about when it could work for you. This is only one example of how it works. There are plenty more. It is powerful and potent.

This is a simple, effective technique that you can implement in the comfort of your own how to increase feelings clarity, calmness, an energised presence, strength, grounding, courage, confidence, connection and love.

Step 3 – Slow down with meditation

How many of you, when you hear this word, wonder what people are talking about? Other people might think, 'How do I do it? I've heard about it, but I just can't seem to get to that Zen place that everybody talks about.'

Meditation is different for every single person. People tend to complicate meditation – but all it is, is an intense, focused attention on one thing.

Through our lives we're so busy and distracted thinking of how to get here and how to get there. We've got to pick this kid up, got to drop this one off, got to run here, run there, be there by that time ... oh yeah, and in the middle of that pay the bills, return emails, Facebook messages, Instagram comments, update Twitter, get fuel, do the grocery shopping and meet your friends and family for coffee ... and then your work day starts!

Meditation will land you deep in your body and slow everything down and give you focused attention on a feeling of gratitude or love or intention.

Don't be fooled into thinking you can only meditate when it's quiet and you're comfortable. You can also get into a meditative state while walking, in shopping malls or coffee shops, or playing with your children. Meditation can be instantaneous.

I don't want to give you more to do, you're all busy people with a lot on your plate, so the difference between my programs and my offerings is that we look at what you're currently doing, and we adapt that.

When first starting to meditate, it's easier to do it in a quiet place. But as you get more practice at it, the same as everything, you'll be able to do it while walking the dog, playing with the kids or at different points throughout your day.

If you're a beginner, start out with a nice, quiet place where you're not feeling any distraction and you can just sink into your body. I've worked with many successful business entrepreneurial women and a lot of us have trouble doing this. Our mind is so full of all the things that we're doing and achieving: conversations, shopping lists, post office visits, children wrangling.

Another interesting pattern in human nature is an association that 'the more I do or the more I achieve, the worthier I'll be'. 'How can I be achieving when I'm sitting doing nothing?' It's this belief that creates questioning and hesitation towards carving out time for yoga or meditation. I have never heard anyone say 'I wish I didn't do that meditation, or go to that yoga class.'

I'd love to share a short meditation that's been really powerful for me; I recommend that you either take this in your own voice or pop over to my website (**www.dianemckendrick.com**) and get the audio for it, then you'll hear it in my voice.

> Slowly close your eyes and start to relax. Imagine a light from the top of your head scanning down over your body. As you scan down over your body, notice if there's any tightness, tension or bits that feel heavy.
>
> Scan from your head, over your eyes, down through your cheeks, over the back of your neck, down through your shoulders, down through your throat, over your upper back and lower back, down through your digestive system, down over your breasts, over your belly button, down through your hips, all the way down the big muscles on the front of your legs, in the back, down through the back of your knees, slowly moving down towards your feet.
>
> Once the light gets to your feet, it's connecting into the universe and it shoots down deep, deep, deep into the core of Mother Earth.
>
> I want you to focus on your breathing, while counting beats. Take a breath in for 3 beats, hold for 2, breathe out for 6. Breathe in 3, hold for 2, and out for 6. Keep up this beautiful, deep yoga breathing and concentrate on your breath. Take it in, deep into your stomach, and breathe out – letting the weight of

the world slip away from your shoulders. With every breath, you feel more relaxed and calmer.

As we progress through the meditation, the numbers will crumble away and you'll just be left with your breath and space. It feels so good to be so connected, so relaxed.

In this beautiful serene state, I'm going to take you for a walk. I want you to walk around on the grass, feeling the grass under your feet and the sun on your face. The temperature is perfect: not too hot, not too cold. As you're walking around on the grass, breathing deep, you come to a river. Beside the river, you're standing on the rocks, which are warm under your feet.

I invite you to imagine a zip from the top of your head, all the way down the middle of your body. You're going to unzip … as you do, your human suit falls to the side. You take a step forward into the water and into the light, where you meet with your soul essence. Where you meet with your soul signature, your light, the melody of your heart and soul.

You're in the nice, cool, water. You can feel your essence dropped into your heart, connected into your soul, and it feels so full. It feels so right. The water's cool as you walk through the river and when you get to the other side, you turn around and see the human suit laying on the ground. The old fragments and pieces of the past, to be taken up and engulfed back into the universe.

As you look down at your hands and your feet and you feel the depth in your heart, you step into the light, walking forward now with compassion, love, clarity and certainty ... just knowing that you're enough, exactly how you are.

I'd like to invite you to take this feeling with you to every interaction, every connection, every phone call, every red light, every meal you prepare and every two year old tantrum. Just know that your soul lessons will never change. Your soul lessons will never change.

You're slowly going to count up to 5 and you're going to come back to the room, feeling rejuvenated and energised. 1, 2, coming back and remembering everything, feeling so relaxed ... 3, 4, open your eyes ... 5.

Spend some time every day focused on your breath and how your body feels. Do this meditation as often as you like.

Acknowledgements

A deep appreciation and expression of love and gratitude to EVERYONE I've crossed paths with over the past thirty-eight years: every conversation, interaction and connection has been the catalyst for this book and has manifested my first book, *Rise UP*, into reality.

Firstly, to my husband.

My best friend, my lover, my confidant and my biggest fan. You believed in me long before I believed in myself. You are the most caring, warm and gentle man. You always hold me in the highest vision of myself.

The first time we locked eyes, I was lost in your gentle, deep blue eyes – I knew I was home. You look into my soul, have my heart and hold my hand – every day I am grateful for you.

Thank you for believing in me on the days I didn't believe in myself. Thank you for always reminding me that I am enough. Thank you for being sturdy and strong, but with softness and grace.

You are my favourite, the kiss to my hug, the seed to my pod. Thank you for taking my hand and standing by my side.

To my children, Ross and Esme, my little people. This book is for you. To remind you that you are PERFECT, whole and complete just the way you are. To dream big and always stay true to you. To be your own observer and be a friend to the voices in your head. My world is a better place because you are in it.

To Michelle, Allan and Andrew, my siblings – my reflections, my courage and my JOY. Every day I thank graciousness that we have this lifetime to enjoy together, to learn, to grow to LOVE together.

And lastly – Mum and Dad. THANK YOU for loving me. Thank you for the tough lessons, for every pair of socks you paired for me, for driving me at 4 am to swimming training and then rocking up with breakfast and taking me to running all before school. Thank you for the sacrifices you made and never speak of. Thank you for the late nights of worry during my delinquent years and giving me a hug when I stumbled in at 6 am, even though you were heartbroken and hurting.

Thank you for waking me up at 11 pm and making me do the dishes because it was 'my turn' and instilling the TEAM mentality.

Thank you for believing in me.

About the Author

Diane McKendrick was born and raised in Ipswich and still resides in Ipswich, Queensland, Australia.

She is the second-eldest of four. Born second to Michelle, her older sister by three years, Diane then graced the world with her presence. Allan was born a few years later and then Andrew joined the family two years after. The awesome foursome are still best friends, business partners and each other's biggest cheerleaders.

A small town girl with a big heart, she was a gifted athlete and by the time she was seventeen, she had represented her state and country for both swimming and running.

Due to an injury, her direction and focus changed; as an eighteen year old she decided to escape the 'expectation' of going to university and backpack around the world for two years.

Being of a naturally shy and timid nature, these two years abroad were very exhilarating, frightening and challenging.

On returning to Australia, Diane got a job as a receptionist and at a shopping centre, spending the next ten years working her way up to Portfolio Manager of several shopping centres.

She was about to move to Sydney to start her new job when she met a man with 'blue as the sea' eyes on the beach on Australia Day and chose her heart over her head. She decided to remain in Brisbane and married Gus in 2010.

In 2012, Ross was born, then Esme popped out on the lounge room floor a few years later. (Thanks to Modern Midwifery for the natural, magical home birth experience.)

Today, Diane lives in Ipswich with her young family and is close to her extended family. She runs a successful holistic health-based organisation with her family and has an international following. She is a personal trainer, NLP practitioner, past life regression therapist, motivational speaker, intuitive healer and host for spiritual retreats.

Diane is a family person who is passionate about bringing the best parts of science, spirituality and soul signatures together to remind humans of their power. To stay true and authentic to yourself and follow your dreams, while filling your cup and being FULL, balanced and aware.

Diane spends her days running national and international Goddess retreats, a DōTERRA Essential Oils business, online coaching and mentoring programs, and writing books.

MORNING MUSINGS

FREE - visit:
www.dianemckendrick.com

Start your day ON PURPOSE to gain clarity and bliss in your life.

Wake up with words of wisdom and morning musings with Diane McKendrick.

WHAT YOU GET:

7 DAYS of FREE AUDIOS

These easy to play, 2 minute audios can be played from your phone to ACTIVATE your true self to start your day with absolute authentic alignment.

Have you waking up ON PURPOSE to live and create the life you deserve and desire.

Help flick you off autopilot and have you feeling focused, harvesting your highest health, catapult you into clarity and ready to dive into the day ahead.

MEET ME ~ 20 MINUTE MASTERMIND

Free 20 minute one-on-one consultation with Diane McKendrick

FREE: Book your spot on my website: **www.dianemckendrick.com**

Love it all so far and not sure where to start ? Book your 20 minute Mastermind with me.

I promise you, after 20 minutes with me, your life will NEVER be the same!

I can HELP you. Please receive this gift and opportunity to maximise your potential. We will spend 20 minutes together and I guarantee that after our session you will have gained more clarity, peace and direction in your life.

BOOK TODAY!

ABOUT MY RETREATS

day spiritual goddess retreats – visit **www.dianemckendrick.com** to see the up coming retreat

ise your vibration, increase your vitality and release the goddess within!

- Woman's circle work
- Breakdown to Breakthrough. Change limiting belief systems and replace with possibility and power
- Vision Boards
- Crystal jewellery making classes
- Meditation
- Camp Fire
- Full plant based menu
- Yoga every morning
- Intuitive healings
- Cacao ceremony
- Mandala drawing
- Sound and Voice healings

this sounds like your JAM - visit **www.dianemckendrick.com** to check dates and book your spot
w. Several are run throughout the year and always sell out so book your spot NOW.

Remember Ring

Channelled & intuitively designed by Dianes sister Michelle Anne, these creations are globally anchoring women to their truth & presence. This jewellery was created to assist its wearer to remember her true self & let her emerge when placing on your finger or around your neck set an intention and with each glimpse throughout the day you will be reminded of your power.

Your healing is the healing of the collective, rise up sister and welcome to the tribe.

WWW.DIANEMCKENDRICK.COM

Diane McKendrick
Author · Speaker · Life Coach

Notes

www.ingramcontent.com/pod-product-compliance
Lightning Source LLC
Chambersburg PA
CBHW021111080526
44587CB00010B/480